The Modern German Novel

THE MODERN GERMAN NOVEL

A SERIES OF STUDIES AND APPRECIATIONS

BY

HARVEY W. HEWETT-THAYER

Essay Index Reprint Series

originally published by

MARSHALL JONES COMPANY

BOOKS FOR LIBRARIES PRESS
FREEPORT, NEW YORK

First published 1924
Reprinted 1967

STANDARD BOOK NUMBER:
8369-0537-7

LIBRARY OF CONGRESS CATALOG CARD NUMBER:
67-23232

PRINTED IN THE UNITED STATES OF AMERICA

TO MY FATHER

FOREWORD

EXCEPT for Fontane, whose novels belong to the last decades of the nineteenth century, and Rosegger, who died during the war, these essays are concerned with the work of living authors. Contemporary literature grows while one is writing about it, faster perhaps than one can keep up with it, certainly so rapidly that it becomes impossible to incorporate references to new work. Since the essays were begun several years ago, Zahn, for example, has published a number of novels, which unquestionably sustain his reputation, though they do not indicate any essential change in the art of his story-telling. Further, many aspects of German life which are reflected in modern fiction have become altered to a degree that a few years ago would have been thought incredible; doubtless at many points in these studies the past tense should be substituted for the present.

That the essays are informative as well as critical arises from the nature of things; in writing of books, particularly of foreign books, which few have read or are perhaps likely to read, one serves a useful purpose by describing what manner of books those are that are worth talking about at all. The paper on "America and Americans in Recent German Fiction" appeared originally in "The Bookman"; the editors have kindly given me their permission to reprint it here.

H. W. H–T.

PRINCETON UNIVERSITY
PRINCETON, NEW JERSEY.
June 1, 1924.

CONTENTS

The Modern German Novel

AMERICA AND AMERICANS IN RE-CENT GERMAN FICTION

IT is now nearly a century since Germany first listened to the story-telling of James Fenimore Cooper. The spell of his genius established the conception of American life as a frontier struggle enlivened by occasional hostilities with pictur-esque savages, — a conception which still persists among the uninformed. German novelists soon tried their hand at American stories in the style of the "Leather-Stocking" series, answering the perpetual human interest in exotic adventures and an aboriginal civilization. This novel of pure adventure was soon followed and accom-panied by the so-called "emigrant" novel in which the focus of interest was fixed on the ex-periences of Germans in finding a new home in the new world, novels which were often written with the confessed purpose of instructing or warning prospective home-seekers; these stories frequently presented the inchoate society of western borderlands with sympathetic insight and a lively humour. To-day, however, the story of frontier life, the Indian or Wild-West tale, is largely of the penny dreadful variety, the product of a German factory or the trans-lation of American wares. The gay covers with their lurid scenes brighten the windows of pro-

1

vincial shops, and, for a few pfennige lure the youth of Germany to a Wild-West thrill and incidentally to a curious view of America.

Yet in fiction which is to challenge the attention of the intelligent, the emphasis on wildness of scenery and stirring adventures, or crude and primitive standards of living, must inevitably grow weaker. America becomes in the course of time the scene of a developing civilization offering noteworthy points of contrast with the old world, which grow more subtle with the increasing stability of the social order. German interest in America is, in part, a natural result of a half-century and more of emigration; indeed it may be said that Germany has felt, through this indirect participation, whether or not with adequate warrant, a kind of proprietary concern in the great American experiment. Sometimes large companies from one community have gone forth to seek homes in a new land. Frenssen in "Die drei Getreuen" (The Three Comrades) gives an account of such a departure, individualizing many of the group, noting their motives in leaving the homeland and their hopes for coming days. The novel as a comprehensive record of German life could not fail to account in some way or other for those Germans who have gone over-seas; it would be inconceivable that Germany's emotional life should bear no marks of their absence. Thus, in novels which otherwise present no American interest, "gone to America" and, perhaps, "lost sight of there" are occasional phrases which record the incompleteness

of the family circle. And these words leave
their trail of pathos over many pages; the exile
becomes absorbed in his new life, and with the
years there comes a diminishing sense of kinship,
a half-forgetfulness or carelessness which distance
engenders despite the effort of our wills. On the
first page of "Jörn Uhl" Frenssen speaks of
Mutter Weisshaar, three of whose children lay
in the churchyard, one in North Sea depths, and
four others lived in America, but two of them
had not written for years. To earlier emigrants
America was primarily a land of economic hope;
in the modern novel it often appears as a refuge
of another kind; it is a place toward which escape is possible out of conditions which restrain
or gall, where life may be attempted again after
all, if not begun anew. Thus it is suggested, for
example, as an asylum for Frenssen's Hans
Thorbecken in "Die Sandgräfin" (The Sand-
Countess), who has quarrelled with his father
and struck him; it is a sanctuary for Zahn's
Vinzenz Püttiner, who loves his brother's wife,
for the hero of Heyse's "Zwei Gefangene"
(Two Prisoners), a rebel against his priestly
vows, or for Dr. Huhn and his foster-daughter in
E. von Wolzogen's "Die Entgleisten" (Wrecked),
when ghosts out of the past pursue them even in
their own innocence and make life on German
soil a torture.

But the German novel represents German
interest in America in other and much less negative ways; it actually goes to America in search
of American material, or it seizes upon that part

of America which American travellers and returning German-Americans bring over, as it were, for the convenient inspection of those who dislike an ocean voyage. Thus with the present generation of novelists we find more and more frequent glimpses of the American scene; the American traveller and the German-American, usually classified indiscriminately as American, grow increasingly prominent among the foreigners introduced into the German novel.

The temptation to derive generalizations from the views of American life thus directly or indirectly presented is obvious and in the main justified. As a rule the German novelist attributes to his American characters those qualities which he thinks peculiarly characteristic of Americans. The American characters appear, at any rate in part, as representatives of a class and not as individuals. As a matter of fact, only the more intimate of our acquaintances appear to us primarily as individuals, and they recede into a class precisely as our acquaintance with them diminishes. Most men of our acquaintance are simply a bundle of class characteristics, plus an indefinite amount of individuality which varies as our nearness to them; we classify thus the plumbers of our experience, the lady school-teachers whom we may meet, the ward politicians with whom we may or may not have dealings. Thus it is with the incidental American in German fiction; he is first and foremost American, and may or may not have interesting human traits of his own.

Much of what might be compiled from German novels to form a composite view of American life and character, as the German novelists conceive them, is manifestly the product of limited observation or indeed of no observation at all. Comment on the external aspect of the American or the qualities of his spirit is often only the handiwork of the imagination aided by a current and persistent tradition. When, for example, Hugo Grob in Zahn's story, "Der andere Weg" (The Other Way), returns after three years in America, he has sacrificed his moustache and wears, "in American fashion," a pointed goatee; the author's experience with Americans is evidently in a certain sense symbolic rather than real.

The legend of the American's love of money and his ruthless pursuit of it has become a conviction among Germans, held with the tenacity of a religious dogma. An absolute absorption in business which blinds to truer values and shrivels the inner life seems a natural corollary. The geography lesson in the German school is the beginning of this belief, and it is held sacred along with the unquestioned verity of the multiplication table.

In his novel "Atlantis" Hauptmann lends the authority of his name to this conception of American ideals. The hero's American experiences begin on the steamship which is bringing him hither. The contemptuous opinion of America and Americans expressed by his fellow passengers form a kind of introduction to the personal impressions

after landing. An armless German acrobat who
is coming to America to fill a music hall engagement thinks America too barren and tiresome even
for a burial place; the American is like a parrot
which ceaselessly repeats the words "dollars and
business" and "business and dollars"; he sees
everything in the world and his fellowmen as well
only as representing a value in dollars. A sculptor from Berlin has ever on his tongue the scorn-
ful epithet "Dollarland." Another voyager remarks that America was founded by thieves, "if
you stretch a tent over it, then you will have the
most comfortable penitentiary in the world." The
inclination not to take these and other similar
opinions seriously because of their source, or the
effort to interpret them as satire on the travellers
who utter them, is checked by the views of the
hero himself and the conclusions to which he
comes before his visit is at an end. To him New
York is possessed by a veritable insanity of greed,
a "wild and shameless scuffle for gain," it is "an
eternal procession, crawling, dancing, leaping after the dollar, the sacrosanct," and all amid a
pandemonium of ear-splitting tumult. That the
topography of New York is at times somewhat
hazy, that express trains thunder over an open
square without any barrier whatever, that nearly
all the important and influential positions not
only in New York but in the whole land are held
by members of the Tammany organization, are
perhaps matters of picturesque inconsequence,
from which inferences should not be drawn; but
the author's general position is not left in doubt.

The most direct and comprehensive denunciation of American hypocrisy, rapacity, and turpi-
tude is involved in the advice given by the hero to
the kindly German physician at Meriden, Con-
necticut, who has spent years in America,—and
it is not to be supposed that Hauptmann singles
out the medical profession in America for particular reprobation. "The Americans have no use
for such men as you," he says, "you can neither
recommend patent medicines to them nor fasten
a poor working-man to his bed with little doses,
using him as a milch cow, when he could be cured
in a week with quinine. You have none of the
characteristics which constitute the nobility of the
standard American. From the American point of
view you are an utter fool, for you are ready to
sacrifice yourself for any poor dog. You must go
back to a land where the nobility of intellect is
still the equal of any other kind of nobility. Don't
stay in this gigantic commercial company, where
art, science, and true culture are for the time being out of place." The doctor makes no effort
to refute this obloquy, though apparently the
words are not received without dissent, for the
doctor loved America and when he put his ear to
the ground, he heard the subterranean music of
future days. Thus the offence of to-day is palliated by the promise of to-morrow.

Rudolf Herzog, who had shown some interest
in America through the Spanish War scenes of
his "Hanseaten," has devoted a recent novel "Das
grosse Heimweh" (The Great Home-sickness)
entirely to German-American problems. His con-

clusions in regard to American life are similar to
Hauptmann's. The general framework of the
story is formed by the journey of a distinguished
German scholar through the United States. He
travels inflamed with the sacredness of his mission,—to arouse the Germans to self-assertion, to
the preservation of the German heritage for the
enrichment of American culture; he urges a close
and abiding relation with the Germany overseas,
and a unified political activity which shall lend
weight to German efforts here and may, in case of
need, be used in favour of the old fatherland.
The desired mingling or amalgamation of the
German elements with the Anglo-American is suggested by a figure which is a variation of the familiar melting pot; German wine is poured into
Tiffany glasses, "the marriage of the noblest with
the noblest." This symbolic act, however, in no
way represents the content of the novel; for the
most part the author is engaged in advertising the
German wines and in finding flaws in Tiffany
glasses. There are in America, the wanderer is
told, only two classes, those with and those without dollars; the latter are recognized by no one
and are hardly taken into account in legislation.
German immigrants rejoice at first in the new
freedom and equality, but later many bite their
lips till they bleed at the remembrance of the land
left behind. Culture is a foreign word which men
here have difficulty in pronouncing; everything is
at present so much more easily arranged by dollars. There is no youth and no idealism.

Bernhard Kellermann's novel "Der Tunnel," a mild sensation of yesterday, presents an imaginary picture of America after the lapse of years, perhaps half a century. A stolid fancy has supplied for future days merely an exaggeration of certain supposedly characteristic aspects of New York life; conspicuous among these, the very essence of American living, are concentration on business success and love of bigness for its own sake. The sky-scrapers have grown taller, the blaze of advertisements more insistent; the speed of transportation has kept pace with the increased intensity of living; the newspapers are more grotesquely personal and sensation-seeking. Over familiar is the emphasis upon the heat of summer and the cold of winter, upon the over-heating of the houses, and the love of big things and of conspicuous splendour.

Yet there are dissentient voices. The author of the "Briefe, die ihn nicht erreichten" (Letters, which did not reach him), for example, acknowledges an "intellectual aristocracy" in whose circles she heard no mention of either money or business. In Herzog's novel, opinions are occasionally expressed which run counter to the general current of disparagement; they are quantitatively insignificant, but they do not allow the conception of American life as totally materialistic to pass unchallenged. A Harvard professor characterizes the American as an idealist even in his business, and the German critic is made to nod a vigorous approval; courtesy is apparently with him a fairer jewel than consistency. Exceptions to Herzog's

general estimate are, however, usually characterized, quite conveniently, as "not American";
places, for example, which appear less crude are
emphatically labelled "not America"; New York
is simply a European suburb on the American con-
tinent; California, land of exotic beauty, has been
dipped in temperament; Boston, with its memories of the Revolution, of poets and thinkers who
have walked her streets, is "not America,"—a
superior, aristocratic spirit, intangible but pervasive, prevails there; Washington in its dignity
and beauty is a place apart. In Kellermann's
story the rich are not unmindful of the poor, and
the socially privileged are ready to surrender
their ease in order to lift the down-trodden and
to bear burdens which are not their own.

It may be worth noting that most nations at
present regard most other nations as deficient in
ideals, as composed largely of narrow-minded
Philistines, shop-keepers and the like, busily engaged in cheating one another and greedily seeking to acquire temporal possessions.

Then, too, in estimating the sway of gross ma-
terialism over American living, a dividing line
may be drawn between American men and American women. To the German observer the American woman is unquestionably a more interesting
phenomenon than the American man. She is regarded as a rather anomalous product of a commercial civilization, and considerable interest inheres in the complexity of her character. She
stands aloof from the market-place and enjoys the
concrete advantages of man's insensate lust for

acquisition. Lack of discipline and the possession
of unrestricted privilege give to the American
woman interesting possibilities which are rare in
continental experience. An educational system
which makes no difference between men and wom-
en may lead the woman who has no professional
purpose to serve into purely capricious pathways
of decorative erudition; unrestrained by practical
considerations, the woman may gain a superficial brilliancy of learning which covers a clut-
tered and untrained mind. The womanly qualities
of unselfishness, devotion, and genuine sentiment
are imperilled by the very independence and ador-
ation which are hers. That neither bubble learning nor heartlessness is thought to be the inevitable result of American training is, however,
amply evidenced, but it is noteworthy that in
many cases German blood or the spell of European tradition has had some share in the redemption.

The heroine of Ompteda's "Der Zeremonien-
meister" (The Master of Ceremonies) is, perhaps, the most flattering portrait in the German
gallery of American women. In beauty of person
and elegance of dress she is the typical American
woman of the continental conception, but the
author has endowed her with unusual qualities of
mind and heart. Even in matters of dress she is
unlike many, since she attains distinction through
simplicity, refinement through unadornment;
there is, however, no unwomanly austerity or
blue-stocking indifference, she is frank in her unaffected desire to please, and her costume is the

result of thought. But vanity and arrogance, the frequent concomitants of American beauty in European eyes, do not appear in the picture. She scorns the flippant gaiety and emancipation of some of her compatriots whom society in Dresden somewhat grudgingly accepts. The breadth of her cosmopolitan culture is often set in contrast to the limitations of ladies in society circles. One cavalry captain expresses his embarrassment in conversing with her; she has no relatives in the army to serve as starting points for harmless chatter on personalities and no matrimonial ambitions to be served by gossip of regimental or court society. Her world is not surrounded by provincial barriers; she is interested in everything,— painting, sculpture, music,—she has read everything; "knows who Dante was, while I merely know that King John translated him and that he always wore a laurel wreath." Nor is there any suspicion of superficiality about her learning or her appreciation of the beautiful; immediate response to the stimulus of allusion does not imply a mere surface readiness. To her the master of ceremonies shows his collections,—paintings, embroideries, porcelains, bronzes, wood-carvings,— the spoils of wide and intelligent seeking; it is with a touch of æsthetic loneliness, for no one, save two professors from the art school, had ever shown any interest in them. With Miss Bancroft he finds the knowledge of an expert,—attributions, schools, influences,—and the taste of an unprofessional connoisseurship.

Her mother is a German-American of American
birth, but to this source her cultivated tastes are
in no way ascribed. Mrs. Bancroft is confessedly
purely practical; she is bored in museums, and at
the opera she investigates the boxes through her
lorgnette, while her daughter does not turn her
eyes from the stage. Yet German culture is not
without its share in shaping Eva's taste. A natural and unexplained predisposition to love things
of beauty has been developed by years of European travel, but to self-trained native endowment
direction has been given, intensity and thorough-
ness have been added, through association with
a young German art critic, the lover whom Eva
has so unhappily misunderstood. It is, however,
not simply her rare intellectual gifts which cap-
tivate the ageing master of ceremonies and win
him for a time to dreams of youth renewed; depth
and sincerity of character, kindliness, tenderness,
sympathetic insight, true womanliness,—all are
hers. So to him that Dresden winter becomes a
kind of reminiscence of Goethe's Marienbad summer.

Thomas Mann's "Königliche Hoheit" (Royal
Highness) also has an American heroine, and of
a somewhat different type. With kindly humour
the novelist sets the stage for his story; it is
the life of a somnolent, unprogressive principality with its stiff but not unkindly forms of
intercourse between a beneficent aristocracy and a
simple, curious, but contented people. Into this
old-fashioned serenity comes Samuel N. Spoelmann, an American multi-millionaire, to drink the

healing waters of the Ditlinden-Quelle. He is physically a very inconspicuous personage, inconspicuously dressed; the crowd at the railway station on his arrival is especially disappointed at his unsmiling face, for local rumour had provided him with front teeth of gold into each one of which a diamond had been set. Spoelmann is a pathetic figure; his incalculable riches bring him neither real happiness nor surcease of pain. He finds a kind of solace in playing the organ, in collecting glass,—he possesses the rarest assemblage in the world,—and in the society of his daughter Imma. Mr. Spoelmann is in no way responsible for the unscrupulous methods by which his adventurous German grandfather founded the family fortune, but lavish gifts to Spoelmann University and other educational institutions or benevolent enterprises fail to placate a resentful American public, and European residence is on the whole more agreeable. Delphinenort, one of the grand-ducal palaces, is in the course of time purchased by the American, this transaction affording considerable temporary relief to the grand-ducal coffers. Popular resentment at the sale of a crown seat is stayed by the acquisition of so splendidly taxable a resident.

The loneliness to which the unpopularity of her father's possessions has banned them, has developed in Imma a peculiarly incisive manner of speaking, and a mocking superiority, which masks her real emotional nature. But Prince Klaus Heinrich, the younger brother of the reigning Grand Duke, falls under the spell of this

exotic personality. She bewilders the poor fascinated prince and twines him about her finger. Of
her favourite study, algebra, he is lamentably
ignorant, and he understands her allusions neither
to the Adirondacks nor to a parallax, though
apparently they sound something alike to him.
Imma exercises a benevolent tyranny over her
father; she enjoys an independence at home and
assumes a freedom abroad which excite surprise
in the "residence." Once this freedom sets the
whole town by the ears. In her devotion to
higher mathematics Imma is attending lectures at
the university, and once happens to be hastening
thither at noon. In front of the ducal palace she
encounters a body of soldiers engaged in the interesting if unimportant spectacle of "changing the
guard." An officer shouts hoarsely to her to
turn back and opposes her progress with the butt
of his rifle; with indignation Imma brushes it
aside and continues to her destination. This lack
of respect for military discipline is viewed in this
happy principality with general merriment.

Imma Spoelmann is racially a very variegated
human being; her grandfather, a German, had
married a Bolivian of Spanish and Indian descent,
and her mother was a German-American who
was half of English blood. Imma tells the prince
that Indian blood is looked upon in America as
a humiliating stain, though likely to be overlooked
when present in small quantities as in her own
case. But in a family whose wealth was so noto-
rious, such matters were sure to be brought up;
amid the insults which sometimes followed her on

the street, she had heard the jibe that she was "coloured." It may be said in passing that the mingling of races in America, real or fancied, is a matter of considerable interest and speculation to the Germans. American characters in one of Spielhagen's novels are presented as interesting racial problems because of their negro blood. That this American girl with her Indian ancestry marries the prince smacks somewhat of the fairy tale. Yet the Spoelmanns lived in princely fashion with liveried servants and in a real palace; there was something quite regal in the general aloofness of their lives, though the park was open to the public as before, in ducal days; and their activities were recorded in the local journal side by side with the happenings at court. Imma visited hospitals and interested herself in various kindly enterprises, and her father supported them with more than regal liberality. What wonder then that the simple folk began to think of Imma as a princess! And since the Grand Duke could at will convert his brother's betrothed into a countess, with promise of "princess" later on, what obstacle could there be to the course of true love? Only Samuel N. Spoelmann indeed, who was possessed with American ideas and had some serious misgivings because "the young man has no real occupation," but he yielded to romance and incidentally saved the finances of the duchy.

Independence may, in certain cases, breed a kind of super-being, beyond good and evil, which cannot be judged by ordinary standards. There emerges an unsexed human, of fascinating loveli-

ness. This harsher conception of American womanhood is presented in Georg Hirschfeld's story
"Der Wirt von Veladuz" (The Landlord of Veladuz). Mrs. Harryson, the daughter of an
American railway king, arrives at the new mountain rival of St. Moritz. A whole retinue of
servants and trunks innumerable accompany her.
She is tall, commanding, of extraordinary beauty
and grace, but hard, imperious, and arrogant;
she even carries a dagger in a gold scabbard at
her belt, and for use, — perhaps a reminder of
her cow-boy descent. Restless in energy, she
knows the whole world, is an intrepid mountain
climber, bent on actual discovery, and has plans
for an expedition to the South Pole. Despite the
three rubies on her fore-finger, she is not vulgar;
she has insight and artistic sense: "What beautiful house is that, that genuine old one?" she asks
with reference to the old inn, now superseded by
the meretricious splendour of the great hotel.
But she has no heart; "the world in which she
lived consisted only of nature and servants." No
one exists for her except in so far as he serves her
or provides diversions for her jaded spirit. She
is pitilessly, brutally cruel, but without malice;
she is far too imperial for that. Lucy, her daughter, is a specimen of the American child, apparently observed somewhat superficially from the
youth which often infest the corridors of continental hotels. She has one supreme quality, malicious cruelty. She treats her little dog with
spiteful ferocity, her over-amiable governess she
beats till the blood flows, and she is actually on

the point of shooting the hotel-keeper with a revolver. This latter prank is regarded by her mother as an expression of her individuality, and, as such, natural and in no way reprehensible. The discipline of business competition will tame American boys, or, at least, convert them to another kind of savagery; society may perform a similar service for the little girls. Mrs. Nelson, the great singer in Sudermann's little story "Die leidende Dritte" (The Other Woman Suffers) is not dissimilar to Mrs. Harryson in her ruthless egotism, but she is less completely a "superwoman"; she has not raised herself entirely above good and evil; she is still aware of distinctions, and openly recognizes them by seeking to manipulate public opinion in her favour.

Absence of an aristocratic body which determines social usages tends to chaos in social conventions, when their existence or validity is at all recognized. Doctrines of freedom and equality lead to a defiance of good manners, since deference to superiors is the source of courtesy. Neglect of decorum is a besetting fault of the young, and the older world looks sometimes with irritated indulgence upon the lapses of our childhood. In Gabriele Reuter's "Episode Hopkins" two young Americans, both destined for the Church, are residing temporarily in Germany for the acquisition of the language and the broadening of their horizons. One of them is a millionaire and the other is a kind of parasitic climber, existing on his friend's generosity, and master of every form of pretence in furthering his own ends. The

young men are from Boston, and the distinction
between Bostonians and other Americans is emphasized. Pride of knightly English ancestry has
given these young republicans a certain arrogance
of bearing, and Harvard has bestowed on them,
in their own view of it at least, "the highest intellectual culture and the patent of good breeding
and fine manners." Quite possibly this is the only
German novel calling such express attention to
the "difference between this venerable institution
and all other American universities." They as-
tonish the Germans by the comprehensiveness of
their culture and the profundity of their philosophical conversation; the comparative narrow-
ness of German clergymen is deprecated. Yet
drawing-room etiquette proves in Germany to be
something of a stumbling-block for both. American indifference is repeatedly attested by their
amazed disapproval of social restrictions. It
may be remarked incidentally that even in cul-
tured Boston the young millionaire's mother does
not allow him to go out at night unattended for
fear of attacks by the proletariat.

The structure of German society, the conventions which govern the relationships between man
and man, rest on a foundation of lingering feud-
alism. Germans assume that American society is
still largely permeated by the spirit of that famous Declaration which began our national life;
only we have accepted certain modifications to
allow for the worship of Mammon. Gabriele
Reuter's "Der Amerikaner" is an entertaining
study of a young German aristocrat who has been

subjected to the influence of American democracy. Fritz, "Der Amerikaner," belongs to a noble family which has long been favoured by association with exalted personages of the local court, that of the duodecimo principality of Langerode-Hirschburg-Nassenstein. The family estate, however, is weighted heavily with mortgages, and Fritz's father is facing disaster, since neither rigid probity of character nor even more rigid observance of courtly etiquette can be converted into acceptable assets. Some years before the opening of the story, Fritz had retired to America because of sundry financial burdens of his own, and now he returns, bringing only the riches of his experience and an interestingly altered point of view. The latter well-nigh paralyzes the family at the very moment of his arrival. A real princess, to whom Fritz's aunt had once been lady-in-waiting, is honouring the family with her presence at luncheon; a more inopportune time for the interposition of American democracy could hardly be imagined. Fritz is refreshingly "American" in his disregard of formalities and enchants the bored old lady by his blithe unconventionality. Seized by an attack of sentimental German homesickness and having no funds for the return journey, Fritz had obtained the privilege of shovelling coal on the steamship, but a happy game of poker on the morning before sailing had provided a first-class ticket and a new suit of clothes. And Fritz never finds any abiding adjustment between the ancient cherished attitude of the family and the now ineradicable freedom of his own way of

thinking. He feels in him nothing of the nobleman who must preserve a distance between himself and the villagers, and he ridicules his brother
who charges him with undermining the authority
of the aristocracy by his inconsequence. His
awakened business sense, his spirit of enterprise,
set on foot a scheme which regenerates the
finances of the family, though he himself has
sometimes a sentimental misgiving at this disturb-
ance of the traditional aloofness; at times a clash
of feelings overwhelms him, which he says is unknown in America, the discord between a desire
for energetic progress and a reverence for hal-
lowed traditions.

If neglect of traditional courtesies and ignorance of immemorial standards are characteristics
of undeveloped childhood, so too, are our lack of
reserve and our tendency to boasting. Childish
also is the emphasis on externals, the curiosity
about one's neighbours, the love of show. Restlessness and lack of application in the accomplishment of serious tasks, especially the intellectual,
are traits which the American shares with the
school-boy of all times and places. The American's quest for culture is regarded as essentially
naïve, though the sincerity of his thirst is sometimes admitted. Real devotion to learning, to
art, as well as to social amenities, is considered
sporadic at present.

The religious life of America is to the average
German a book with seven seals. The multitudinous sects, corresponding to the vagaries of
individual belief and experience, are spoken of

with amazement or with condescending humour. The ease with which adherents are found for a new "denomination" is illustrated in one of Heinrich Seidel's stories where there is mention of a melancholy individual, abnormally fond of eel-soup, who emigrates to America and founds there a "nice, little, new religion." Herzog's wanderer finds that religion is merely a matter of fashion with most Americans. This implies that change of faith is not a solemn step resulting from altered convictions; on the contrary, the crowd follows eagerly those who have the ingenuity to devise new and striking dogmas or observances, and readily forsakes the favoured sect when fashion decrees. With women in particular, he says, religion is a pleasing variety of sport. That business ends are sought through scrupulous church attendance seems natural when once business is accepted as the one underlying, solidifying principle of society. In spite of the variety of faith and the chameleon-like changes, which would seem to challenge anything like intolerant assurance, Americans are generally credited with an unyielding orthodoxy and an active bigotry. In Spielhagen's novel referred to above, a German idealist had founded in New York a school for orphan children, but fanatical clergymen, finding his views on the Bible unsound, used the opportunity of a street brawl and incited the mob to destroy the institution.

In external forms of her political life America is less fantastically unique. The political affairs of the Republic are more extensively and accu-

rately reported in the German newspapers than
the whims of religious dissent. For the politics
of America affect the economic life of Europe;
this shrinking of the world into economic interdependence is suggested in Wolfgang Kirchbach's
novel of the outcast and vagabond "Das Leben
auf der Walze" (Life on the Tramp), where
the working classes resentfully charge the McKin-
ley Bill with the responsibility for their woes.
There is, too, a certain parity of conditions as far
as governmental functions are, or seem to be,
within the competence of the people, and this
supplies a readier basis for understanding. Since
politics are the affair of all, interest in political
matters is assumed to be characteristic of all. At
the same time stress is laid upon the sinister aspects of public life in America, the participation
in politics for the sake of gain, the corruption in
high places. That some men make politics a business, that many take their business into politics,
is a natural result of a civilization where business
is the chief concern of life.

Rarely in the old world do opposites stand in
such striking juxtaposition as in America; matters
there have through the passing of the centuries
found their relative positions by an unerring
principle like that of specific gravity, while here
society and its concerns are in a state of flux. The
German novelist notes, with baffled effort at understanding or reconciliation, the contrasts and
contradictions of American life. It is only a step
from the splendour of Fifth Avenue to the squalor of the slums; it may be, in another sense, only

a few months or years of struggle or luck from the tenements to the "Avenue." Similar contrasts and contradictions are found in the composite make-up of American character; nowhere does character react more directly and completely to external conditions. The environment is one of stupendous change; the chief characteristic of the external aspect of America, so far as it is subject to man's control, is its impermanence, and human qualities seem here to be peculiarly susceptible to the might of altered circumstance. In this very mutability of men and things lies, it may be, from the European point of view, the hope of our salvation, that is, eventually a modified conformity to established standards. There is, for example, a tacit satisfaction discernible in the recorded observation that our population shows a tendency to divide into classes.

To see ourselves as others see us is commonly valued as a wholesome though supposedly unattainable experience. It may be less efficient a corrective, if we know that the "others" have never really seen us and merely think they have, if they judge us from some old photograph which never did us justice. If we know their deficiencies as observers, we can discount such items of the picture as we may choose to disapprove. To look one's self squarely in the mirror is to most people a humiliating and disconcerting experience; if the mirror is convex or concave the experience may be hilariously diverting, but the distortion of the mirror is convex or concave, the experience unconscious or which we ordinarily refuse to see,

and the diversion becomes wholesomely edifying.
It is an experience of this sort which awaits the
American who seeks a portrait of our national
physiognomy in the pages of the German novel.

THEODOR FONTANE THE REALIST

THOSE whom the gods love do not all die young: indeed some favoured spirits seem to be granted a special bounty of years, in order that they may still find their own destined way of serving their fellow-men. Thus with some authors, who come late, but happily not too late, into their kingdoms, we associate a certain mellowness, a breadth of perspective, and a charity that come with the years; by their genial wisdom and kindly forbearance life is tempered and enriched. To this group of the best-beloved Theodor Fontane belongs.

After a long and varied experience, as apothecary and journalist, traveller, ballad-writer, and historian, Fontane published his first novel when he was in his sixtieth year. It was in 1878 that this first story, "Vor dem Sturm" (Before the Storm) appeared, and before his death in 1898, Fontane had a full score of novels to his credit, leaving one or two in pathetic incompleteness. "Vor dem Sturm" is an historical novel, conceived in the Scott tradition, which had long been powerful in Germany, and was, perhaps, transmitted to Fontane through Scott's chief German follower, Willibald Alexis. Fontane tells, however, of the immediate past, of a time within the memories of his older contemporaries; his novel is a careful and substantial picture of Prussia in the years immediately preceding the revolt against Napoleon's sovereignty. After a brief period of

experimentation, Fontane found his own special
field, the novel of contemporary social life in Berlin and in the Prussian territory tributary to the
capital; despite occasional excursions into other
regions, Fontane made this type of story characteristically his own.

At first glance perhaps, the chief characteristic
of Fontane's novels may seem to be the extraordinary fidelity and completeness with which contemporary life is reproduced. The contemporary
background in many of its aspects, the topics of
thought forced upon society by external conditions are reflected in the lives and especially in
the conversations of his characters. His novels
abound in references to that which is even minutely contemporary and local. Sweets are procured
"of course" from a well-known confectioner, certain popular restaurants or variety theatres in
Berlin are spoken of familiarly; a local pastor in
the Mark is compared with a famous court
preacher. One might be tempted to condemn
Fontane's frequent inclusion of such references as
akin to the practice of employing recondite allusion or quotation in order to gain the favour of
the initiated by flattering their vanity. The time
will come,— is perhaps fast upon us,— when a
certain type of reader, irritated by the possibility
of anything escaping him, will demand annotated
editions of Fontane's stories; for, unfortunately,
confectioners die and court preachers as well, and
go to their reward; social conditions shift, and
familiar subjects of discussion become remote and
academic. Fontane's practice in this respect is,

however, quite in keeping with the habit of the intimate *raconteur;* discussion or allusion may, for the initiated, open flood-gates of significant reminiscence, but, take it all in all, neither discussion nor allusion bears any essential relation to the real enjoyment of the story, for Fontane establishes the centre of interest in less transitory things.

Though he sees the world about him with unfailing accuracy and is aware of its problems, Fontane is too genuine an artist, or, in other words, too natural a story-teller, to allow his epic purpose to be deflected into sociological byways. His stories do not, except indirectly, present the effects of a transitory environment on the lives of men and women, nor do they engage in the purposeful depiction of a social order, which may or may not be in need of the physician. Like the surface of a lake his characters mirror the clouds above them, are ruffled by the winds of to-day; their motives are modified by contemporary prejudices. But the lake is not essentially changed by cloud or wind. Fontane is primarily concerned with deeper and more elemental matters; he uses the contemporary and the temporary, but only as a means through which the changeless things are discussed.

In other words, Fontane's stories are not "novels with a purpose," and it may be maintained that a part of Fontane's claim to abiding popularity as a writer of fiction is based on the fact that he did not attach his fortunes to the exposition of a particular class or problem, to any plan for social

regeneration. Novels thus conceived, though unquestionably valuable to future historians of social conditions as mines of investigation, begin, in
just such measure as the temporary considerations
outweigh the permanent and elemental, to recede
into the dust of literary archæology. The more
ambitious novels of Spielhagen, for example, are
conscious efforts to grasp the meaning of restricted periods of German cultural history; social and
historical conditions which are just fading into
retrospect are held firm for our inspection and
illustrated by certain characters chosen to react
to such a stimulus as the novelist wishes to describe. Spielhagen's novels have long since begun
their pilgrimage to the untroubled top-shelves.
The same is largely true of Paul Lindau's stories
of Berlin life; the consciousness of the transitional period in the life of the capital led Lindau,
and others indeed, to incorporate in fiction certain
contemporary phases and tendencies of the life
about them. But the later student of social history may find a more trustworthy store of material for the reconstruction of past society in the
incidental and the casual than in the purposeful
and the schematic. Vision is rarely vouchsafed
to those who try overhard to see.

In the last analysis, Fontane is concerned with
little less than the personal relationships of one
human being to another, relationships that are
usually conceived in a very elemental or even
primitive sense. The individual will may indeed
be in conflict with the world-will as registered in
the standardized impulses and inhibitions of or-

ganized society, and it may be necessary to lay weight upon certain peculiarities of the social organism which are characteristic of a certain time, yet the novelist, after due recognition of accessory circumstance, pursues his quarry to its lair, the recesses of the soul, where one personality meets and enters into relationship with another personality. Like the great master craftsmen of his trade, he strips man to his elemental nakedness, where human spirit meets human spirit in problems essentially unchanged by time and place since the angel with the flaming sword stood at the gate of paradise.

With unwearying reiteration, then, Fontane seeks concrete expression of certain problems which in one form or another seem inalienable from human living as long as men and women retain those characteristics which make them men and women. In the first place, a large fraction of his work is resolvable, upon analysis, into the formula which has been conveniently called the "triangle." These stories, possessing thus a fundamental similarity of plot, differ nevertheless among themselves, and naturally, for otherwise only one of them would be worth telling. Fontane grapples, for example, with the theme made memorable by the story of Anna Karenina; a woman is married to a man considerably older than herself; it is a marriage of convenience, arranged by others on some other principle than on that mutual attraction which deepens into love,— and, with the addition of a third person, the material for tragedy becomes complete. It was with a

novel of this sort, "L'Adultera,"— his fourth
story,— that Fontane first portrayed contemporary life in Berlin.

Kommerzienrat Ezechiel van der Straaten, with
the suspicion of Hebrew blood not entirely set at
rest, is a successful man of business; he displays
a ready intelligence and possesses a very respectable amount of miscellaneous information on
other than business topics. In spite of the introductory analysis of his character, which fills the
first pages,— a procedure that Fontane later very
largely discards,— the novelist almost allows him
to deceive the reader in the earlier scenes; his
worldly poise, his cultivated tastes, his ready and
almost adroit conversational gifts, form a cleverly wrought veneer for the homely, crude, and
unlovely substance which hides beneath. Thus he,
appears at a dinner-party which introduces the
reader to the set in which the Van der Straatens
move, but the reader is permitted to accompany
the guests on their way home, and the polished
surface of Van der Straaten's appearance is subjected to a searching examination. Frau Van der
Straaten was Melanie de Caparoux, a French
Swiss, considerably younger than her husband.
Outwardly, at least, their married life of ten years
has been normally happy and unruffled; two children have been born to them. Then a disturbing
presence is introduced in the person of Ebenezer
Rubehn, a business connection of Van der Straaten; he is a man of the world, has lived much
abroad, in London, Paris, and New York; he
now seeks a closer acquaintance with the business

world of Berlin, in order to found there a branch
of his father's Frankfort house. Considerations
of business relationship, assuming the guise of
hospitality, make Rubehn a guest in the Van der
Straaten household. This act of courtesy is perhaps the host's dramatic guilt. Both Melanie
and Rubehn struggle against the destiny that grips
them; Melanie had never really loved her husband; she had simply taken him as a part of the
general scheme of things beyond her control, to
which she was largely indifferent but which supplied a method of living which the world as she
knew it simply took for granted. The days of
deepening affection lead to open acknowledgment
and then to flight; the latter, strangely enough,
does not finally take place without a frank discussion between husband and wife, now really that
no more. After a brief Italian journey, the transgressors return to Berlin, and with the courage
of bravado, seek to rehabilitate themselves in the
society of the capital. The meeting between Melanie and the children whom she has forsaken tests
the novelist's skill in conceiving and handling an
emotional and tensely tragic scene without allowing it to degenerate into melodrama. The renegade wife feels reconciled to her course only when
a reversal of fortune forces her to stand beside
the husband of her choice in adversity as well as
in prosperity, to work, and to suffer the common
lot of womankind.

Fontane's next novel presents interesting parallels and divergences. Graf Petöfy, whose name
supplies the title of the book, is a middle-aged

Hungarian nobleman, and a Roman Catholic; he
marries a winsome young actress, the daughter of
a Protestant pastor in a town by the Baltic Sea,—
a staggering array of contrasts! Through this
new arrangement of qualities and conditions, providing for a new inter-action of character, the
material is obviously calculated to bear a different
emotional burden from that observed in "L'Adultera." It has, further, the sources of another
kind of pathos, perhaps a deeper kind of pathos,
because the tragic elements are more purely personal and evenly distributed, each bearing consciously his or her share. The situation which
develops is not due to an obsolete but persistent
method of arranging marriages, a system of governing without the consent of the governed, but
the two people concerned go into their matrimonial venture of their own choice and with open
eyes. The independence and the sophistications
of her profession obviously prevent the actress
from following any other motives than to secure
for herself the maximum of life's satisfactions.
Though she is not without ambition, there is no
vulgar self-seeking in her acceptance of the suit;
she is fascinated by the aristocratic bearing and
the courtly love-making of the count, unconsciously perhaps also by the subtle charm of his Hungarian blood. She is sincere in her action, recognizes the seeming irreconcilabilities of the situation, but is confident that their case will be the
"exception." Though the doors of Viennese society are open to him, the count is lonely and
bored; his sister, the wise and patient Countess

Judith von Gelder, perceives the unreality of his love, and tells him that he reminds her of a prince who wishes to engage a reader or perhaps a cellist. But the count does not listen to her warning. The account of the weeks directly following the marriage and the retirement of the count and his bride to the Hungarian estates is skilfully managed to provide indications of the coming disaster. The count outlines the life they are to lead, a life of mutual consideration, regulated, carefully divided, allowing for daily hours of companionship, a plan which is the result of thought, and is promulgated with confidence, though in its very essence it blocked at the outset that unconscious melting of interests, that merging of personality, which marks the real union of man and wife. A nephew of the count, young Egon, comes for a visit; the count begins to suspect the young people of fondness for one another's society, watches them for a time, and then, in full realization of his hopeless mistake, he takes his own life. But his wife, chastened and sobered by the old man's tragedy, resolves to give her life to her people, the half-feudal dependants on the estate of which she has now become mistress.

Though "Cecile" presents essentially the same situation, a woman and two men, the problem is altered sufficiently to provide new finenesses of adjustment, of motives, and of characterization. The finger-prints of character are as individual and as subtly discriminated as those which physically mark every man as essentially unique; hence the permutations and combinations of such units form infinite series. At Thale in the Harz Mountains, Gordon, a civil engineer of wide wanderings, meets Colonel St. Armand and his wife Cecile. Through a common participation in the mild diversions of Thale, this acquaintance develops into friendship. From the beginning Gordon is aware of something abnormal in St. Armand and his wife; something unexplained which separates them from their fellows. His increasing interest in Cecile is accompanied by various speculations as to her past; he is surprised at her want of drawing-room information — she relapses into embarrassed silence when the conversation takes a turn involving matters of art or letters; how can she be so accustomed to social usages and yet so naïve? She is apparently afraid of something, perhaps of her husband, St. Armand? Months afterwards Gordon seeks out the St. Armands in Berlin, and through Fontane's stock device of the dinner party, he is introduced to their circle. From members of the latter and through a letter from his sister, he learns the story of Cecile's past. Through the conscienceless greed of her mother, a widow of questioned reputation, Cecile had, as a girl, been positioned as "reader" to a prince, whose mistress she became, then after his death she became in turn the mistress of his successor. On the death of the second prince, she came back to her mother's home, where she met Colonel St. Armand, and they became engaged. One of St. Armand's subordinate officers branded this betrothal as unworthy of St. Armand's military position; the latter challenged his detractor to a

duel and killed him. St. Armand then retired
from the army, and Cecile, renouncing the Roman
Catholic faith, married him. It is a loveless marriage now on both sides; St. Armand, embittered
that it has cost him his career, becomes petulant
and morose; Cecile is hypersensitive, secretive,
and irritatingly humble; they keep only an outward show. The tragedy develops after Gordon's reception of this information; indeed, the
predominant interest in the story, which Fontane
himself apparently felt and which he communi-
cates to the reader, lies in the subtle difference in
Gordon's attitude toward Cecile after his entering
into possession of these facts. With fine intuition
Cecile herself knows that he has been informed;
with a sensitiveness born of watching other people's conduct toward her, she notes the slight low-
ering of his tone, and openly charges him with
it. Gordon even descends to a rudeness of which
the Colonel himself must take notice, for Gordon
seems to insult him, in ignoring the safeguards
which marriage has placed about his wife. He
challenges Gordon to a duel, and Gordon falls.
To Cecile the Colonel sends a message to meet
him on the Riviera, but it is too late; Cecile has
already taken her own life.

In its main outlines, that is, in the triangular
problem, Fontane's masterpiece, "Effi Briest," is
similar to these stories, is closest perhaps to
"L'Adultera." The Briests are an old family of
the Mark, now occupying a manor-house built in
the early seventeenth century. At the opening
of the story, Effi, a girl of sixteen, is playing in

the garden with some companions of her own age;
half child, half woman, she romps at hide-and-
seek. From all this careless merriment she is
summoned to a meeting with the bridegroom to
whose suit her parents have given their approval,
Baron Innstetten, aged thirty-eight and a former
suitor of her mother's. At the very moment when
she advances to meet him, comes the impatient
call of her playmates in the garden: "Effi, come!"
calling her back to girlhood, and irresponsibility.
In one of his letters Fontane said that he had
written the whole story about the pathos of this
unanswered call.

Effi acquiesces in her parents' plans; she makes
no protest,— it might seem petty to object to the
interruption of the game,— and she has no other
basis for disapproval; a long conversation with
her mother discloses her utter ignorance of love.
Then follow the marriage, the wedding journey
to Munich and Italy, and the homeward trip to
Innstetten's place near the Baltic Sea. In chapters notable alike for their penetration and for
their delicacy and restraint, the novelist ushers
Effi into her new home. Innstetten is "Landrat,"
a man of conscientious, perhaps over-conscientious
devotion to duty; work at his office demands his
constant presence. Thus, after the early novelty
has ceased to exert its influence, the first touch of
homesickness has yielded, Effi is enveloped in the
drab dreariness of un-enlivened routine. The
local society of town and country-side offers to the
youthful bride very little of friendly intercourse;
it is, to tell the truth, far too formal and grown-

up. Then too, she has a superstitious fear of the very house in which she lives; she is tortured by the weird story of the Chinese servant of an old sea-captain and the mysterious disappearance of the captain's granddaughter: Effi's weakness in yielding to this ghostly awe brings into her married life the first real harshness of misunderstanding. Summer brings the city people to the shore, and the arrival of a baby seems to promise reality to the united interests of man and wife. But Innstetten's absorption in the fulfillment of official obligations becomes more complete when pointed by the prospect of advancement. Effi is even more alone. Major Crampas, the new commandant of the local militia, becomes an occasional visitor to the house; he rides with Effi over the dunes; Effi is very fond of riding, and Innstetten is far too busy for it. A kind of comradeship develops, which after a time becomes sufficiently intimate to allow Innstetten to be a topic of discussion between them. This step toward a dangerous intimacy, with all that it involves, is emphasized also in "L'Adultera." Once Crampas suggests that the ghost of the Chinaman is merely a part of an educational scheme which Innstetten has concocted. Effi does not understand at first, but, once apprehended, the idea rankles and will not down. Effi has misgivings about her friendship with Crampas, and there is evidence of her purposeful avoidance of him. But Innstetten is rewarded for his zeal by a post in the ministry in Berlin; in Effi's parting lines to Crampas, the whole truth of their relationship is revealed.

Years go by, and then, in Effi's absence, Innstetten accidentally discovers letters of fatal incrim-
ination,— Fontane is incidentally quite unabashed
in his use of so thread-bare an accident to develop
his plot,— he goes back to the Baltic sea-port
town; a duel is arranged, and Crampas falls.
Innstetten then obtains a divorce. Effi is refused
an asylum even by her parents, the sting of pub-
licity is too keen. She rents a modest apartment
in Berlin, and lives there, accompanied by old
Roswitha, who had been the faithful nurse of her
little girl and is now not less faithful in the unhappiness and the desolation of her mistress.
Once Effi sees her daughter on the street; an
uncontrollable longing possesses her, and, through
the influence of old-time friends, a meeting is
arranged, a meeting which is but an incomparably
more pathetic repetition of a similar scene in
"L'Adultera." Death comes to Effi as a welcome
release, but happily not until her father and
mother, relenting, have taken Effi back to her
childhood's home and to the old-time love.

The story of "Effi Briest" is doubtless the chief
support of those who find in Fontane the most
distinguished German follower of Flaubert. In
certain conspicuous elements of plot, the resemblance to "Madame Bovary" is not to be denied;
Fontane agrees too with the French master, here
as elsewhere, in making his narrative primarily
an accumulation of commonplace, so-called "realistic" materials, but, take it all in all, the temper
of the two stories is widely divergent, largely

through the infusion of Fontane's sympathetic personality.

Fontane's third venture in fiction, the story of "Ellernklipp," is worth a passing word, since, though coming in his early period of experimentation, it evidences his interest in the problem of the "triangle," before he had found his characteristic field in the life of contemporary Berlin. In "Ellernklipp" Fontane shapes the problem to a thing of tragic intensity by making the two lovers father and son; and in addition, the story is removed from the reserve and constraint of social circles into primitive surroundings. A gloomy forest in the Harz Mountains is the scene, and the protagonists are the forester, his son, and an orphan girl who had been brought up in their home. With great discretion the novelist shows the development of the rivalry, the passion of the ageing forester, the vigour of full flame, and the more idyllic devotion of the younger man,— till at last the father murders the son, and then marries the girl. A strange wedded life then follows, — resignation and a kind of filial respect on her part, and on his, a tortured conscience and the fear of being found out.

In two important novels, "Schach von Wuthenow" and "Unwiederbringlich" (Beyond Recall), Fontane turns the triangle about and places a man in relationship to two women. "Schach von Wuthenow" is, incidentally, Fontane's most noteworthy historical novel. "Vor dem Sturm," though vivid and convincing as a portrayal of an historical period, is, as a story, clumsy and crude; "Grete Minde" forms the novelist's only attempt to enliven a remoter epoch, a period far beyond the memory of his contemporaries, but the pitiful little tragedy is mainly a personal one, and reflects only somewhat dimly the peculiar temper of times which immediately preceded the Thirty Years' War; and in "Ellernklipp," though supposedly a story of the later eighteenth century, only a few insignificant references connect the action with an historical epoch. "Schach von Wuthenow," however, is a consummate example of the real historical novel; historical events are not used by the novelist simply to make easy adventures for his characters or to supply an extraneous interest, but the basic principles which determined the course of history are evolved in the characters and the incidents of the narrative. Like "Vor dem Sturm," this story deals only with the immediate past; the scene is laid in Berlin, during the months before the battle of Jena; an element of historical truth most forcibly emphasized is the shrivelling conception of military pride and soldierly honour which had worked like dry-rot in the Prussian army.

Since the hero wavers in his allegiance between a beautiful mother and her plain, but interesting daughter, one might call this tale the obverse of "Ellernklipp." Frau von Carayon and her daughter, Viktorine, belong to the so-called "French Colony" in Berlin, exemplifying Fontane's fondness for characters taken from that section of the population whence he himself had sprung. Just as Melanie in "L'Adultera" is irritated by her

husband's lack of innate refinement, so Schach, as
an officer in a smart regiment, is assured that the
smallpox marks on Viktorine's face, her facial
"abnormality" as he calls it, would worm into
his life's peace, were they to be man and wife.
While Schach dilly-dallies in the friendship of the
two ladies, not really hesitating between them,
because unconscious of any necessity of choosing,
or of putting this relation upon any other footing,
he is led by the passion of a moment to compro-
mise the daughter in such a way that the mother
demands of him the legitimatizing of their fault.
This is the test of Schach's character. He is a
soldier of the times, and his ideas of honour are
bound up in external things; an overwhelming
horror of ridicule among his regimental comrades
seizes him; he pictures to himself the malicious
jibes at the immaculate cavalier who thus allowed
himself to become entangled; and seeking the seclusion of his country estate, he broods with distaste over the seemingly endless and monotonous
years which await him there when this scandal
has forced his resignation from the army. Though
impeccable as an officer, he is a moral coward.
Frau von Carayon, misinterpreting his absence,
seeks the aid of the king and queen. Schach regards the ensuing desire of the king as an inviolable order, and the marriage takes place, but he
shoots himself on the night after the wedding.
Fontane uses two letters to close the story, one
from a friend of Schach's, giving the public view
of the tragedy, and pressing home as well the
symptomatic qualities of the situation; the later

Fontane, with a finer sense of fitness, would have left these matters to the reader's inference. The other letter is from Viktorine in Rome, living in her memories, and seeking consolation in the church of her forefathers.

"Unwiederbringlich" is a not dissimilar tragedy. The hero, a country nobleman in Denmark, a man in whom the fires of life still burn, is attracted by the somewhat conscious charms of a coquette at court, while his wife, grown relatively older, supersensitive, morbidly and introspectively pious, whiles away the barren hours at home; a break with the coquette brings the husband back home again, but nothing can restore the relations of other days, and the wife finds her only refuge in the sea.

But in two of Fontane's most forceful and appealing stories, he forsakes the "triangle" and presents a very different problem of relationship between men and women. The organization of society which recognizes and sanctions a rigid stratification into classes, presenting smooth cleavage surfaces, is an anomalous product of the evolutionary process, since it involves the frequent clash between elemental laws and artificial rubrics. The established order, for example, separates those who, in accordance with primitive human laws, might form the most perfect union, and in turn, unites irreconcilables; the latent tragedy in such separations, without emphasis indeed upon the converse in disparate union, is the theme of "Irrungen, Wirrungen" and "Stine."

"Irrungen, Wirrungen" (Errors and Entangle-
ments) is a very modern version of that age-old
theme, the relationship of a young nobleman to
a girl of the people; its modernity consists, in
part at any rate, in the utter absence of heroics,
in the simple acquiescence in things as they are,
without bitterness and without rebellion or remorse. The heroine, Lene Nimptsch, lives with
her foster-mother, who is a laundress, and Lene
herself does linen embroidery. Accident brings
a young nobleman, Botho von Rienäcker, across
her path; he comes and then comes again. With
Lene, her foster-mother, and their neighbours, he
sloughs off the artificialities of his world and
shares in the homely pleasures of the proletariat,
delighting immeasurably in their kindly humour
and, in view of the limitations of their experience,
sensibly surprised and perplexed at the maturity
of their wisdom; it fascinates him as the mystery
of childhood's intuitions. Fontane never leaves
the reader in any doubt as to the direction which
the story is to take, though the exact method and
the kind of outcome he does not prematurely disclose. It cannot become a "Gretchen" tragedy;
Lene is far too much a child of her sophisticated
generation; there is no deception either on her
part or on that of her lover, and Lene's mother
has only a word of approval: "It's no harm,
child, before one knows it, one is old," a fairly
prevalent sentiment in her circles. Despite her
lowly origins and the obvious limitations of her
training, Lene is incomparably the stronger of the
two lovers, and she makes neither hopes nor

dreams out of the relationship; the thought of
its transitoriness occasionally masters her; —
"Which rowboat shall we take?" asks Botho,
"the 'Trout' or 'Hope'?" and Lene answers:
"The 'Trout,' of course, what have we to do with
hope?" When Botho, unconscious of the futility
of it all, talks of his mother and his family as he
might if Lene were really his betrothed, she interrupts him, reminding him that he will go away
and leave her some day: "It is just as I say . . .
you will, because you must. You think every day:
'If she were only a countess!' but it is too late
for that." And it is, once again, a modern version of the "King's Children" separated by the
great waters, but with a very modern difference,
for both, when they think of it, realize the im-
passability of the great deep, the untold years of
class prejudice and class distinction. And it all
came as it had to come. Botho's own world called
him; the fortunes of the family depended on his
marrying wealth; arrangements are made for
him, and he follows his destiny. The parting
scene between the two lovers is one of deepest
pathos, particularly in its brevity and restraint.
But Fontane's story does not end here; Botho is
not unhappy in his married life; though his wife
lacks real depth of character, is incorrigibly shallow perhaps, she is still of the kind which disarms
criticism, and begets affection. Lene too is sought
in marriage by an honest working-man whom she
accepts after a frank confession of her past. One
of the most remarkable scenes in modern fiction
is the call which Lene's suitor makes on Baron

Botho; though, in view of the moral code prevalent among the continental proletariat, it is perhaps hardly supported by plausible motives, it is
in itself peculiarly effective.

"Stine" was planned before "Irrungen, Wirrungen," but was finished only when "Irrungen,
Wirrungen" had gained an audience for the novel
treatment of an old theme. It is, as Fontane
said, a kind of pendant to the story of Botho and
Lene. Stine is a working-woman, no longer
young. She is employed in an embroidery shop,
but for the most part in "piece-work" which she
brings home. She has quarters in the very modest flat of the Polzins,— Herr Polzin is a plum-
ber. Downstairs is the home of her widowed
sister Frau Pittelkow, who, after various vicissitudes, is now the mistress of an elderly nobleman.
Here, Count Waldemar, the nephew of the latter,
meets Stine and becomes interested in her; for a
time he cherishes the ambition to take her away
from what he considers her degrading environment. But the count's well-meant philanthropy
is never put into execution; it recoils upon himself, for he finds that Stine is incomparably more
able to help him than he is to help her. Her little
journey in the world has given her poise, an intelligent, clear-visioned appreciation of human
strength and human weakness, a philosophy of
living to which he listens in pitiful envy. "A poor,
sick chicken" Frau Pittelkow calls him; tempera-
mentally unfitted for the life which his rank demands of him, physically below normal, he wants
only to love and be loved, to be guided by an-

other's wisdom. To Stine, bending over her embroidery-frame, he comes again and again for courage, for judgment and affection. He even proposes marriage to Stine and informs his incredulous uncle of his intention, but Stine herself decides the matter; she is quite aware that she can never be a countess, just as little as her lover can abjure his title and his blood. The seas that lie between are too deep and wide, and the count finds no pathway to peace but in suicide.

The tone of the novel is muffled, subdued, the very antithesis of hysteria, a plaintive melody in a minor key, broken now and then by passages of merriment; otherwise it might have become a fervid indictment of a social order which cramps and starves those men and women whom a social order might be supposed to serve.

In "Frau Jenny Treibel" a difference in social class, operating as a barrier to matrimony, is turned rather to comedy, partly because the difference itself seems quite unsubstantial, and hence not to be taken seriously, and partly because the tragic potentialities receive little stimulus from the lovers themselves, with whom passion hardly rises above the first warmth of spring. Frau Jenny is the wife of a rich manufacturer whose activities have gained him the title of *Kommerzienrat*. In the enjoyment of her wealth and her title she succeeds in blinding her new environment and herself even, for the most part, to certain unpleasant truths of the long ago, when, as plebeian Jenny Bürstenbinder, she actually assisted now and then behind the counter of her father's little shop. She has become a spacious and pervasive personality, dispensing hospitality with the elegance appropriate to her station, and effusing dignity and refinement. While stressing the simple sincerity of her emotions, the tenderness of her sentiments, she is at heart cold and almost ruthless, acting ever with an eye to the main advantage; she deceives nearly every one through her masterly blandishments and cajolery, the few who resist she browbeats into submission, and others, gifted with perceptive powers sufficient to comprehend her, stand aghast at her successes, or, diverted by the comedy of it all, refrain from disturbing the rarity of the spectacle. As an example of the successful *bourgeoise* Frau Jenny is unsurpassed in fiction. In a much lowlier sphere, Frau Wolf, the thieving washer-woman in Hauptmann's "Biberpelz" is closely akin to her.

In her progress from poverty to opulence, she has preserved one old-time friendship; she cherishes a tender regard for Professor Schmidt, once a suitor for the hand of Jenny Bürstenbinder and now a teacher in a "Gymnasium," and for his daughter Corinna. The latter's sprightliness and charm win her a position at the Treibel table even at times when the presence of those near the throne gives the gossip of court personalities a flavour of reality. Corinna makes up her mind to marry Leopold Treibel, Frau Jenny's second son, and quite unblushingly contrives to have him propose to her. Leopold has courage enough to confront his mother with this single unpremeditated act of independence and maintains his reso-

lution for a time in the face of her "Thou shalt
not." But Frau Jenny has other plans for Leopold; she has already indignantly rejected a
scheme for exposing the weakness of his heart
to the charms of his sister-in-law's sister, Hilde-
gard Munk, despite the averred relationship of
the Munk family to the Danish aristocracy; — a
baroness, or the daughter of a privy councillor or
of a court preacher, are not beyond the reach of
her dreams, and she is not of a mind to consent to
anything so absurd as Leopold's project. But,
as the Schmidts' housekeeper phrased it, Leopold
was more afraid of his mother than he was in
love with Corinna, so he remains practically his
mother's prisoner, communicating with Corinna
through secret letters of devotion. Corinna, however, wearies of the monotony of these missives,
and marries her cousin Marcel, who has long
loved her. Directly on hearing of Leopold's indis-
cretion, Frau Jenny has immediate recourse to
the discarded plan for a union with the house of
Munk, taking it as an effective remedy for Leopold's ridiculous fancy. In this she is successful.

This is comedy doubtless, but there is something else marking the substance, something which
at first seems akin to cynicism, but though sham
and self-seeking unquestionably gain their ends,
or at least a part of them, one hesitates to call
the outcome cynical; the humour is too kindly
and the chastisement too gentle. Frau Jenny,
further, does not pass beyond the reach of our
sympathy, and she accepts a despised surrogate
for her ultimate ambition; then, after all, the

marriage which she prevents, really promised less in life's satisfactions than the two which form its substitutes.

The extraordinarily simple outline to which the plot of any one of these novels could be reduced, — in "Effi Briest," for example, a single brief sentence,—is witness to Fontane's comparative indifference to external happenings in unfolding the lives of his characters. It may be acknowledged, however, that one or two of his minor stories present some complexity of plot and make use of thrilling and perhaps somewhat melodramatic scenes. At the beginning of "Quitt," the murder of a forester, the revenge for a personal grievance, is projected against the gloom of night and forest. But the youthful murderer escapes to America, and the burden of the story then becomes the ennobling of character and the expiation of transgression, till guilt is finally purged away when the wounded transgressor dies in forest loneliness, the woods resounding to his cries, even as his victim had died years before,— an ending, which, frankly, borders on the theatrical. But between the stirring scenes with which the novel begins and the reminiscent tragedy in the forest lie the quiet pages of normal experience, which tests and develops character. "Unter'm Birnbaum" (Under the Pear-tree) is also the story of a crime. An inn-keeper who is in financial straits, murders a guest and then by crafty plot he succeeds for a time in silencing suspicion, but "Die Sonne bringt es an den Tag" (The sun will bring it to light) is the refrain which haunts the book, and irresistibly the truth is disclosed. "Unter'm Birnbaum" is a cleverly contrived web of events, provoking a tense interest in the outcome; in no other story does Fontane so nearly approach the novel of incident.

At the opposite pole from these two novels lie Fontane's last two completed stories, "Die Poggenpuhls" and "Der Stechlin," neither of which contains the related sequence of events which we normally call a plot. The former is a refreshing and engaging series of pictures of the old-fashioned gentry, now impoverished but making a pathetically brave show at points of contact with a pushing and successful *bourgeoisie*. In "Der Stechlin" Fontane presents a portrait, full-length indeed, of a Brandenburg country gentleman and his household, together with sundry unexciting experiences of his only son when bent on matrimony. Though it is the longest of Fontane's novels, there is hardly more of plot or circumstance than this.

Mid-way between the two extremes, between "Unter'm Birnbaum," for example, and "Die Poggenpuhls" stands the typical novel of Fontane. It possesses, to be sure, a very definite interest of plot, but the emphasis is laid elsewhere. Fontane is primarily bent on showing how in the lives he traces, certain native qualities are influenced by conditions and circumstances, perhaps largely of an adventitious origin, and how the two, nevertheless, combine to control conduct and thus to determine destiny. The substance of his novels is very largely made up of everyday occurrences, the multifarious but inconspicuous incidents with which the average day, and hence the accumulated months and years slip by. To him the most absorbing spectacle in life is the interplay of character and conduct, and this is a matter of everyday experience; it is not reserved for the great crises, nor is it, to the seeing eye, as profoundly interesting at those points where passions flare up and consume, as it is on the soberer levels where action is normal, and perhaps unconscious or not premeditated. In many cases, for example, Fontane ignores completely those climaxes of action on which another and lesser master might have lavished his talents. The process which leads to the critical moment, to the breach of recognized standards, or the development of character which follows as the resultant of it, the influence on character of the consciousness of dereliction,— are to Fontane infinitely more interesting than the crises themselves. The dramatic in the novel is rarely a lure to Fontane.

As a realist he selects his material from "real life," but his realism does not consist in the purposeful selection of the commonplace as such; he does not with unpitying cynicism call attention to the trivialities of life as man's chief concern, his employments as petty, and his troubles as insignificant. As suggested, he prefers the seemingly commonplace as superior material for his purposes. With rare discrimination he selects and accumulates such details and incidents as show qualities of character or disclose incipient changes of character, or, perhaps, betray potential misunderstandings in the relationships between men and women,— "the little rift within the lute." Effi Briest on her wedding journey writes to her mother of their visit to the Pinakothek in Munich and of her husband's desire to go over to the other museum, "which I won't name, because I am in doubt as to the spelling, and I don't want to ask him." It is, of course, not Effi's orthographic incompetence which Fontane would suggest here as a future cause of marital infelicity; it is the childish fear of her grown-up husband, the lack of comradeship between husband and wife. Graf Waldemar consults his uncle concerning the preposterous marriage with Stine. The old servant Johann has stood outside and listened; he holds Waldemar's coat in readiness and is punctilious in his service, "but the emphatic silence which he preserved seemed to express his own disapproval." He had been long enough in the service of Count Hardern to think even more rigidly than his master about *mésalliances*. Poor Grete Minde, after the years of her vagabondage, returns to her brother's house, which had once been her father's and her own. She enters the outside hall, from which in the old-fashioned house, the doors opened into the living rooms of the ground-floor; here everything is as it used to be, the great chests and wardrobes in their accustomed places,— "only the swallows' nests which clung to the great crossbeam right and left had been removed." Grete notes the subtle change, the malign influence of her sister-in-law: "the house has become inhospitable," she says.

With tremulous emotion Frau Jenny Treibel speaks to Corinna of the Professor's early verses to her, a legacy of his student days: "I've kept them to this very day," she says, "and when my heart is heavy, I take the little book, which originally had a blue cover (I've had it bound now in green morocco), and take my seat by the window and look into our garden, and have my fill of silent weeping, quite solitary, so that no one may see, least of all Herr Treibel or the children. O Youth! My dear Corinna, you have no idea what a treasure youth is!" Frau Jenny's inmost self is revealed by this account of her tears, in the light of the accompanying parenthesis.

Even as the typical substance of Fontane's novels is simple and everyday, so is his method of using it direct and unaffected. His characters meet in everyday ways in the routine of life, the ordinary round of neighbourly visits in town and country, the picnics, the different social affairs, varying in pretension according to the wealth and social position of those concerned,— in other words, at normal work and play. Fontane is particularly fond of the dinner-party as a meeting-place for his men and women; here in conversation they disclose themselves; then afterwards he contrives a continuation of the process by making the prominent characters the subject of discussion after the company has broken up into groups. Thus the novels of Fontane have been called "conversation" novels. This is a strictly realistic method; our opinions of other people are largely formed by what they say or by what

is said of them by those who know them, only
now and then do people really do anything worth
mentioning. Sometimes indeed Fontane may be
fairly charged with violating the probabilities
both in the length of the discourses which he
credits to his characters and the generosity with
which he parcels out to them his own morsels of
penetrating and sententious wisdom. Other realists, Meredith, for example, have erred even more
seriously in this wise.

This natural and indirect method of character
portrayal Fontane nearly always prefers to direct analysis. Not only is the realism of the story
enhanced through this strictly realistic method,
but negatively, that is, through the comparative
absence of direct analysis of character, the novel
gains in vital interest. To just such a degree as
he employs pure analysis, perhaps even the more
acute the analysis, the more does the novelist
transfer the human interest of the story to the
intellect, and distinctly to the detriment of the
novel in its total appeal. Our interest in people
is a curious and unstable compound of the intellectual and the emotional; it is rarely commanding if it is preponderatingly a matter of the intellect. Fulness of life is not granted to those
whose companionships are purely of the mind,
in which the heart does not inexplicably have its
share. Nor is there any material difference when
we seek companionships in books; our use of
books supplies simply a vicarious enlargement of
our human experience. The persistent analyst
tends to exhibit his characters as specimens of his

own virtuosity, to learn to know them is perhaps
a stimulating intellectual experience, but they are
not the men and women whom we really know,
for knowledge is not of the mind alone.

Though Fontane in general seeks his material
in normal human experience, according to the
realist's creed, one hesitates at times to accept
certain passages as reconcilable with the typical
practice of the realists. For example, the novelist displays not infrequently,— notably in "Ellernklipp," an attitude toward external nature which
one is accustomed to associate with romantic fiction; nature is presented as an interpreter of the
mind of man and links her moods in sympathy
with his. But more conspicuous still is Fontane's
use of symbols and premonitions, a habit which
seems distinctly a survival of romantic story-telling. In one novel after another there is a significant repetition of certain phrases; snatches of
song are introduced which are instinct with foreboding and which recur with fateful reminiscence,
welding the substance of the story more closely
together. This practice of Fontane's has been
likened to Wagner's use of the "leitmotiv."
Often this "leitmotiv" consists of a single foreshadowing suggestion, interwoven with the substance of happy days. It is often akin to the
dramatic irony of classic tragedy, consisting
merely of a fateful ambiguity; the words are
meant by the speaker in one sense but are clearly
or vaguely apprehended by the reader as permit-
ting of another meaning. The novelist plays with
words which may or may not be interpreted as

presaging the future. He introduces hints to
which the reader turns back in memory, even perhaps as the characters themselves recall later the
warning guide-post which was unnoted at the
time. Fontane understood well that trick by
which the reader is brought into a peculiarly sympathetic relationship with the characters of a
novel, simply through an identity of memory.

Fontane's employment of this device is usually
highly effective. In his first novel, "Vor dem
Sturm," an inscription on a tomb makes a deep
impression on the hero, and its enigmatical meaning as applied to his fortunes is disclosed in the
unfolding of the story; perhaps at this early stage
of Fontane's work,— in view of his literary pedi-
gree,— this inscription is a reminiscence of the
prophetic verses in "Guy Mannering." In "Unwiederbringlich" the "leitmotiv" is a stanza of a
pensive, melancholy song; the unhappy countess
hears the words in an early chapter, they are
stamped on her memory, and she leaves them behind as her only coherent message when she seeks
in the sea the rest which the lines seemed to
promise. In the pathetic little story of "Grete
Minde," the heroine returns to the church after
her father's funeral; the evening glow illumines
the interior as with fire, and Grete flees from the
building in a kind of nameless terror. At the end
of the story, the wanderer, now returned to her
old home, looks down from the church tower upon
the sea of flames beneath her, the substance of
her revenge. Only through remembrance does
the reader perceive the significance of the earlier

scene. The device as used in "L'Adultera" is certainly less successful: Van der Straaten purchases a reproduction of Tintoretto's picture of the woman taken in sin, and hangs it on the wall, as a kind of symbolic warning. Hence Fontane's scheme becomes simply a direct announcement of the events which are to follow. The failure of the device is not that such a disclosure robs the story of its hold on the reader; one is not led on in such a novel by the mere desire to learn the outcome of a tangle; one is concerned with the development of the characters and of their relations to one another, and the author is undoubtedly justified in warning us as to what the characters are going to do, in order that we may be the more intent on the main problem, the process by which they are led to it. Though Van der Straaten's act is superbly indicative of his character, suggesting his lack of real refinement, his essential brutality, the very use of the "leitmotiv" seems to partake of his brutality, to be equally crude and bald. But such errors of taste are not common in Fontane.

In spite of our first impressions, Fontane's use of the "leitmotiv" is not really inconsistent with realism. The content of our everyday is fertile in material for foreboding. Indisputably that man has lost his peace of mind, if not his mental and emotional balance, who begins to associate the innocent ambiguities of to-day with a possible interpretation for the morrow. But what is madness for the individual in his normal relationship to his own life, may quite reasonably be within

the province of the novelist, even of the realistic
novelist. Out of the manifold incidents which
make up our days, he simply selects certain elements, ordinarily overlooked and forgotten,
which cast their shadows into the future.

Fontane's natural attitude of mind made him
receptive to the doctrines of naturalism, when
that revolutionary movement was first inaugurated. He expressed, indeed, his sympathy with the
propaganda of the naturalists, and commended
their purpose, as they enunciated it,— to revital-
ize literature through a rejection of the artificial
and conventional, and especially by the employment in literary work of those scientific methods
which had been so long successfully tested in the
acquisition of knowledge in natural science. But
Fontane was never so enamoured of the new
theory as to yield to it his personal devotion; he
never became so purely objective in his work as to
regard his characters as biological specimens,
whose pleasures and pains were only of interest
as they might afford material for generalizations
on the phenomena of human life. He never denied the sanction of the selective process, and he
emphasized the right of the artist to select the
beautiful rather than the ugly, for both are a
part of life.

Indeed behind half the confident dogmatism of
the naturalists, who insist on scientific, that is,
objective treatment, lies the simple and by no
means novel effort to attain the illusion of reality.
In the whole checkered history of criticism, there
has been no more fallacious theory than the as-

sumption that the illusion of reality in a work of literature is enhanced by the so-called "objectivity" of the author. In the eighteenth century, the semblance of reality was often sought in a peculiarly naïve fashion; — the novelist tried to mask the products of his imagination by assuming the rôle of editor, collector, or publisher of letters, diaries, or papers; a frequent fragmentariness or incompleteness was thus easily excused, and the incapacity of the author was covered by the suggestion of his irresponsibility,— at the same time the method seemed to contribute to the reality of the impression. For the most part, all of these devices, suggesting reality through accounting for the provenance of material, are as transparent and conventional as a stage drop; they really deceive no one, and influence no one.

The later nineteenth century conceived the principle of objectivity and proceeded to exploit it; only by objective methods, it was held, could the novelist place real men and women in real situations. The theorist who derives such a principle by logical process and then assumes its validity is ignoring the evidence of experience. It is equally a scientific method of attaining truth to consult the accumulated experience of those who read books. One might ask of one's own experience:— is the sense of reality in imagined character and circumstance lessened or not through subjective treatment on the part of the novelist? Are the characters who live immortally for us through the creative fiat of genius in any way connected with the question of subjectivity or objectivity?

The questioning of our experience meets only one answer: the illusion of reality is maintained or forfeited entirely apart from this problem. The novelist may be a perpetual companion throughout his book, commenting on the characters, openly sympathizing with them or scolding them. He may even take us with him into his creative workshop and discuss with us his own perplexities as to character or plot,— and yet in no way impair the reality of the illusion. Conversely, an attitude of strict scientific detachment in no way secures a semblance of the real. The practice of the masters in writing the master novels, infinitely various, of course, would yield a kind of empirical rule, although it would be hard to formulate and might be so inconclusive that it would be of little value when we had laboriously achieved it. But, without endeavouring to forecast the findings of such an effort, there would surely be much to say in favour of the type of novel which carries the novelist along as a kind of "super-cargo"; he is always unobtrusive, but he is always there, and can tell the passengers, not too insistently of course, that the voyage after all has some other purpose than to provide a mere pastime for tourists. It is in this sense perhaps that Fontane is present in his books; the novelist constantly betrays his personal attitude toward the characters to which he has given life: he accompanies their fortunes with evident affection and sympathy, particularly in their loneliness and their shattered happiness; with emotion he tells of wasted and blighted lives, of the perennial enigmas of human living.

Yet Fontane is only indirectly a moralist, and he is, in the stricter sense, not a philosopher at all. Fontane has come to his own conclusions with reference to life; that cannot be gainsaid; some of his estimates of life are easily inferable from his stories, but they are implicit and not explicit. Fontane looked out upon the world with clear penetrating eyes, and he recorded his impressions with unusual fidelity; the material of his novels is made up from his accumulated observations, recreated into life by the power of his imagination. And the novelist's attitude toward life is obtained in the same realistic way; it is a deduction, his own deduction, from observed phenomena. In it neither religion nor metaphysics plays any appreciable part. He does not start from the concept of divine order or interest. If he believes in God, it is essentially the God of the pragmatists, coloured perhaps with a tinge of poetic pantheism; for his inspection of human phenomena favours the belief in God as a workable hypothesis,— it would be a still sorrier world without it,— and the mass of things beyond our understanding implies a power beyond ourselves, which, whether or not "it makes for righteousness" or in any way "works together for good," must be more than mere chance. There is no such thing as chance, Fontane says. Fontane's views have the obvious advantages and limitations of his method of acquiring them; the deductive view of life is prone to be more fragmentary than the inductive; it is easier to apply an accepted theory to phenomena than to derive a workable theory from their multiplicity. If then, we may derive from Fontane only fragments of a moral system, scraps of scattered comment which take the form of interpretation or precept, there is at any rate one unifying principle in his attitude, his sympathetic charity for erring humanity. He spreads a robe of kindliness to cover the multitude of our transgressions.

Though Fontane's novels, practically all of them, present certain deviations from accepted moral standards, the novelist neither condemns nor condones; he is indignant neither at the individuals whose lives are blotted with irregularities, nor with the general make-up of society which allows or haply even fosters such delinquency. He does not stamp Frau Pittelkow as a moral coward because she accepts an easier way of existence than to work for the support of herself and her children, nor does he present her as pathetically ignorant of the right pathway, or gloss her fault with false sentiment. The sin of Effi Briest ruined her own chance of happiness, of satisfaction in motherhood, or in social life; it dimmed the sunshine for all who loved her, but Fontane has no word of scorn or condemnation. Even for Frau Jenny Treibel, whose fundamental insincerity of character tends to block the happiness of others, he has an amused and quizzical tolerance. Politics as a branch of ethics absorbed much of Fontane's keenest thinking, and his novels bear constant witness to his interest, but they are utterly void of anything resembling political propaganda. As Fontane is kind to human frailty, he looks in gentle forbearance upon the vagaries, the inconsistencies, the dogmatics of the political enthusiasts. In an election for the Diet, Count Stechlin, the very embodiment of class pride, is defeated by a social democrat; as he drives home in a blistering humour, he finds one of his proletarian opponents lying drunk by the way-side; not only does he take him into his carriage but he supplies a material gift for the future well-being of his foe,— but he excludes remorselessly from his house a young physician who has embraced the principles of social democracy. Politics are to Fontane a quite unclarified branch of moral philosophy; they illustrate admirably the inherent capacity of the human mind for error and inconsequence.

Fontane yields naturally to that fatalistic interpretation of life which tends to characterize those who take a serious view of man's living but who have no steadying influence of religious faith to act as an interpreter of the otherwise incomprehensible. "What happened was only what was destined to happen," expressed or implied, is the underlying and accepted fact for all his occurrences; this is ever on the lips of his characters as upon his own. But fatalism is in Fontane, not the grandiose spectre of the ancients, nor the petty demon of the fate-dramatists; it is rather a kind of reluctant acknowledgment that the interacting forces of character and circumstance bring about inevitable results, that guilt demands an unfailing recompense, that a mistake can never really be rectified. Such a fatalism is the foe of all heroics, of all older forms of heroism. Despite the suffering and pain or renunciation, particularly in Fontane's women, there is little of thrilling martyrdom about it all; martyrdom implies a "cause," even if it is an unworthy one. Such a fatalistic conception of life engenders in lesser minds, the average man with the average vision, an indifferent attitude toward goals and purposes; of many of Fontane's characters one could repeat what is told of the unhappy Crampas: "He enjoys life, but at the same time is indifferent to it. He takes everything as it comes along and yet he knows that there isn't much to it after all."

And yet Fontane does not allow his fatalistic determinism to become a sour or embittered pessimism; he says himself that pessimism is a matter of temperament; his own temperament was sweet and wholesome, and though nature endowed him with a keen vision for man's inadequacies, for the sources and the substance of man's unhappiness, the total result of his observations is not a cheerless waste. "The result of life, however poor it is, is still always better than it really ought to have been," is, even if a little paradoxical, a characteristic bit of his thinking. In the end he does not fill us with uneasiness about the human animal in his upward strivings, he will not with Mephistopheles compare him to a grasshopper,

"That springing flies, and flying springs,
And in the grass the same old ditty sings."

His findings are, indeed, of a nature to give us
pause, but though the happiness which supposedly
is the legitimate pursuit of man is really unattainable, "all great happiness is a mere fairy-tale,"—
the sum total of human accomplishment in character and in deeds born of character is not discreditable.

But upon the wreckage and the losses Fontane
looks with a kind of wistful resignation, which
supplies a lyric undertone of melancholy even to
his merriment. Fontane's novels are serious if
not sombre books; the genial personality of their
author, his tenderness, his sympathy with man in
his uncertain strivings, even his humour, cannot
make them otherwise. His novels, it may be said
again, are the expression of keen observation and
mature thinking,—the voice of one who has "kept
watch o'er man's mortality," and who has attained the relative calm of harboured waters. But
it is not the calm of an Olympian serenity; it is,
at best, the calm of ripened art, which is as yet
incomplete, for it sees only through a glass darkly,
but has begun to note the presence of the eternal
in the transitory. Thus Fontane is not only a close
observer and a recorder of German life during a
span of years at the century's end; his stories are
records of human experience in qualities which
know neither time nor place. In this, it may be,
lies their abiding worth.

NATURALISM AND THE GERMAN ZOLA

YOUTH is ever restive under the restraints of tradition, and the history of art is punctuated with rebellions which youthful hotspurs have inaugurated. In the last decades of the nineteenth century, the men of "Youngest Germany" repudiated the literary work and the ideals of the previous generation as conventional and anæmic, and sought to create a new literature fashioned after the needs and the wisdom of a new day. Fortunately, as it seemed, a method of revitalizing literature was simply waiting to be used. In this respect they were more fortunate than their predecessors of a century before, who, starting out on a similar project, had little to propel them except their youthful enthusiasm and a certain indiscriminate dissatisfaction with life and letters. The men of this later "Storm and Stress" had a much more definite programme since they had acquired a new way of thinking which might serve as a method of approach to a new criticism of life.

Science looked through a microscope and observed the daily life of the amœba; the domestic habits of the garden worm were analyzed and tabulated. Alluring experiments seemed then possible through manipulation of environmental or hereditary conditions; the worm might be sluggish or appreciably gay in varying circumstances, and because the worm's span of life is brief, generation after generation could pass in review, and the appearance of atavistic traits could be ascertained. The results of such observations were recorded, and then deductions were drawn. Why were not all these processes of investigation immediately applicable to the phenomena of human life, to society, and its institutions, to the relationships between man and man? The practice of literature might become a kind of biological experimentation. Recognizing the law of cause and effect,—every cause working unfailingly to a commensurate effect,—the novelist or dramatist could then plot the human course with the exactness of the physicist determining the resultant of interacting forces; that is, when he had once stated completely the two dominating factors of heredity and environment. The man of letters, after observing, recording, and tabulating, makes his modest contribution to scientific truth.

This mutinous outbreak, like certain other movements in German art and literature, was by no means entirely indigenous. However native and local the stimulus to rebellion may have been, the theory of reform through an application of scientific methods came largely from without. The precept and, in a lesser degree, the example of Zola were determinative. In the early eighties Zola had published his familiar thesis called "Le Roman Expérimental." In the essays which make up this treatise, the scientific methods of the biological laboratory were recommended to the novelist, and the exaltation of the novelist to the rank of a scientist through essential identity of function was postulated as a theory for a new estimate of literary values. "Youngest Germany" was disposed to take Zola at his word.

In one of his critical essays, however, written ten years and more before this, Zola had defined a work of literary art in terms which it is difficult to reconcile with the theories of "Le Roman Expérimental." He said: "a work of art is a corner of the world or creation seen through a temperament." The irreconcilability of this dictum with a theory of literature as a branch of natural science is obvious. Temperament in the novelist would seem to be essentially identical with the so-called personal equation of the scientist. But the latter institutes the most rigid self-discipline to eliminate the personal equation; he carries out the most elaborate system of counter-experiments to correct an error of a thousandth part of a millimeter in the observations of his microscope, lest such an error might perhaps be traced to a source peculiar to himself. The personal equation is the very devil of the laboratory; every attempt is made to exorcise it. What has temperament to do in the workroom of the scientific novelist? In practice, at any rate, Zola did not reject his earlier conception of literary art. His preparatory investigations may have been conducted in accord with scientific principles, but the novels themselves are strongly infused with his personality, are interwoven with his sympathies and his prepossessions; and this remains true of the stories which, in view of his statement of principles, one might be justified in call-

ing specimens of work performed in his laboratory. In spite of his theories, Zola is farther than
many another novelist from the scientific objectivity of the chemist who experiments with carbo-
hydrates and hydrosulphides without evincing any
partiality for the one or the other. As a scientific
novelist, Zola was not an entirely trustworthy
guide.

Both as a protest against the artificial and conventional and as an effort to realize Zola's new
and promising conception of literature, some of
the German rebels made interesting experiments
with scientific methods. But, however enthusi-
astically these literary scientists accepted the alluring theory, most of them in practice interpreted the new creed much as Zola seems to have
done, namely, as a statement of belief, more or
less reserved for times of self-examination or
public confession but less conspicuously determinative in daily conduct. For a time, unquestionably,
they endeavoured to view the phenomena of human life in a scientific spirit, but, after a comparatively brief period of devout conviction, most
of them found it more convenient to abandon the
arduous methods of the scientific laboratory. In
the technique of their work, the naturalists were,
for the most part, content with an accented realism; the substance of their books, expressed in
terms of character and event, was to a very large
extent merely the material long used by the so-
called realists, but in the presentation of character, its sources and its development they stressed
the fundamental scientific principles, and they

sought to relate their various happenings to exact laws of causation.

But, though quantitatively speaking, much of the material in the new fiction presented nothing foreign to the realists of earlier days, the influence of Zola is manifest in a certain extension of permissible themes. Science is essentially democratic; there is no hierarchy among the subjects for investigation in the biological laboratory,— the worm and the primate stand on the same level before the principle of science for science's sake. So the new group of men of letters turned for a time, with the zest of discoverers in unknown lands, to those fields of human life from which the law of standardized beauty had excluded them, the sordid, the unlovely, and the outcast. In the new æsthetics, one of their number maintained, there is no distinction between the death of the greatest hero and the birth-throes of a cow. Hitherto, poverty and misery had lain by the wayside, and literature had passed by with averted eyes. If these iconoclasts wallowed in the mire for a brief space, it was a kind of exaggerated defiance of established precedents, a protest against prettiness and prudishness in literature. Guidance towards these unused realms of human material came obviously from Russia as well as from France.

In view of Zola's relationship to the beginnings of German naturalism, it might be expected that the naturalists would choose the novel for their chief form of expression; and further, because of its greater flexibility, the novel would seem to be a promising field for experimentation. The more memorable works of naturalism lie, however, in the field of the drama. The conviction that the drama is unapproachably the highest form of literary art is a German prepossession, and the success of any literary movement which is acquired solely or primarily in other fields would be stamped as only half a success. It may be noted also that at this time the growing power and authority of Ibsen's plays, both as to their content and their method, tended to increase the prestige of the drama as the supreme method of literary expression. In the drama too, certain limitations inherent in the form render experimentation a less hazardous undertaking; the scientific comprehensiveness demanded by the naturalist's creed is bound in the drama by barriers of time, for the drama is constructed with a view to stage production, and the men and women who see it must be released sooner or later in order that the world's work may not suffer unduly on the following day. On the other hand, the novel recognizes no limits save the patience of the reader and the qualms of the publisher. In the naturalistic novel, if scientific methods be followed consistently, every force which has entered into the moulding of character must be accounted for; the scientist cannot ignore any factor however remote in time or space; each character is a part of all that he has seen or heard, and all that he has seen or heard is essential to a complete statement of character or of deeds which grow out of character. Obviously a naturalistic novel, completely and comprehensively fashioned,

would be a *monstrum*. In the novels of the naturalistic school, a touch of common sense, combined with a certain timidity before so vast an
enterprise, saved the novelist from consistency.
The most significant experiments in the technique of novel-writing were those contained in
the work of Arno Holz and his friend Johannes
Schlaf. Arno Holz was a chief apostle of the
new gospel, and the two friends collaborated in
a volume entitled "Neue Gleise" (New Pathways), in which they offered specimens of new
methods in narrative and drama. Several of the
pieces in the volume had been published separ-
ately, previous to their incorporation with the
new material of "Neue Gleise." One of the
earlier pieces "Papa Hamlet" was one of the most
successful literary hoaxes of modern times. A
slender volume appeared bearing that title and
containing three sketches which were attributed
to a Norwegian author, Bjarne P. Holmsen; the
translator, Dr. Bruno Franzius, supplied an
introduction, putting forward the outstanding
facts of Holmsen's life and work; this foreword
was given a baffling semblance of reality not only
by the completeness of detail but through references in foot-notes. The latter were calculated
to disarm all scepticism. The authors, in·reprint-
ing "Papa Hamlet" in "Neue Gleise," jeered
merrily at press and public, which had fallen into
their trap, and published extracts from a score of
reviews. They italicized the passages which particularly delighted them, such as comments on the
"visible efforts of the translator," and in general,

took a not unwarranted satisfaction in the success of the little trick.

The technique of the three sketches which made up "Papa Hamlet" and of the others which were added to form the volume of "Neue Gleise" is somewhat varied, some of them displaying more strikingly than others the innovations and experiments of a new style. The story entitled "Die papierne Passion" may serve as an example of adventure in naturalism. It was written before "Papa Hamlet," but was first published in "Neue Gleise." A novelty of method is, in the first place, attempted in the typography; in external appearance the sketch resembles, strictly speaking, neither the novel nor the drama, at first sight giving rather the suggestion of the latter. Narration and description are printed in small type, as is common in the stage directions in a printed play; conversation is given in a larger font; the occasional absence of complete sentence structure in the narrative and descriptive parts agrees also with the technique of stage directions, but the identity of the speaker in the recorded conversations is indicated only through statements in the narrative elements, in which there is obvious effort to avoid the conventional "said he" of older narrative. The authors do not designate the speaker through marginal reference as is customary in the drama. The attempt to avoid in this way the familiar external conventions of the novel and the drama is in the end a considerable annoyance to the reader; pages of conversation without adequate indication of the identity of the speaker, other than is naturally inferable from an alternation of two people speaking, make an unwarranted demand on the reader's concentration; he gets lost in the tangle. But, in creating a new art, an author must take some risks.

The argument of the story, if it can be called that, is very simple. A lodging-house keeper in a wretched little flat, up four flights, sits in her kitchen, preparing the evening meal. Two of her lodgers come in, impecunious and flippant-minded students, and they are joined by a ragged, down-at-the-heel old vagabond. The old woman is a curious compound of kindliness and brutality; the latter quality is evinced primarily, and not in words alone, toward twelve-year-old Wally, who is one of the eleven illegitimate children of her sister. An ale house on the ground floor furnishes a very audible racket at times; a factory across a narrow court supplies an insistent buzz as an accompaniment to the conversation; further enlivenment is provided by shrieks for help, which come from below, where a drunkard is killing his wife, and by the sound of boots thrown against the wall in the neighbouring tenement. Old Kopelke, the vagabond, cuts from a newspaper the figures of Christ's Passion, the cross, the two thieves, and other elements of the gospel narrative,— a kind of silhouette play. Wally roguishly blows the figures this way and that on the table and about the room; Old Kopelke rolls a paper lamp lighter out of the Cross, and lights his cigar, whilst one of the students twists the two disciples of Emmaus between his fingers.

The scientific method as here applied consists in a rigid reproduction ɔf that which the senses apprehend, and of nothing else; what the eye can see is described with great exactitude and completeness; what the ear can hear is given as by a sensitive phonographic cylinder; not only is the dialect reproduced with phonetic accuracy, but the broken sentences, the half-words, the inarticulate mutterings, which no dictionary records, but which constitute a part of every man's vocabulary. The sense of smell is also involved in the narrative, though possibly not premeditated, through the odor of onions and coffee. There is no comment on the part of the writers, no criticism or interpretation; they have become a recording machine of scientific exactness. They essay no explication of mental or emotional states as the causes of action; apparently they do not trust themselves in fields which lie too close to temperamental or subjective influences. They would insist that they know nothing of what lies within the mind of the characters, they put down what they have seen and heard without definition or gloss. They have happened in upon this scene and have transcribed it for us. Obviously the authors would repudiate with scorn the witless suggestion that some symbolic interpretation might be attached to the paper figures of the Passion.

Incomparably more moving, because associated with deeper emotions, is the short sketch entitled "Ein Tod" (A Death). Two students watch through the long night till a comrade, mortally wounded in a duel, dies at dawn. The pathos of

this death-bed scene is intensified by the arrival
of the youth's mother at the very moment of his
passing; then too, a neighbouring lodger, provided with odd habits,— which are difficult to explain as pure chance,—plays an old folk-ballad on
his violin as a greeting to the coming dawn, and
incidentally furnishing an effective accompaniment to the wounded man's last moments.
Through its emphasis on homely details, by its
excursions into irrelevancies, the method of the
naturalist throws into relief the ever-recurrent
tragedy of death, and stresses in this way the
pitiful relationships of men and women to the
petty concrete things of life, doubly insignificant
and everyday now in the direct presence of the
coming negation,— the things of time brought
into sudden contrast with the great uncharted
spaces. Though the method is new, the use of
this contrast is not a discovery of the naturalists;
death has often been made to seem more poignant, the suddenness or completeness of the break
more vivid, by reference to the insignificant
things which will be touched and seen no more.
Despite his frequent mawkishness, Dickens was
a master of this device. The poet often uses it:—
"Your hands once touched this table and this
        silver,
And I have seen your fingers hold this glass.
These things do not remember you, Beloved,
And yet your touch upon them will not pass."
In all sober-mindedness, and with all allowance
for the play of chance in the midst of realities,
one perceives art rather than science in some of

the essentials and in more of the accessories of
"Ein Tod." A romantic sentimentalism has apparently crept in through the laboratory key-hole.

After the associated experiment of "Neue
Gleise," Holz deserted story-telling, but Schlaf
has persisted, though forsaking in the main the
pathways of stylistic innovation, and in his more
important work becoming a conditional apostate
to the naturalistic creed of himself and his friend.
The sketches to which he gave the title "In
Dingsda" (At What's its Name) and the later
companion volume "Stille Welten, Neue Stimmun-
gen aus Dingsda" (Quiet Worlds, New Musings
from What's its Name) are highly subjective
and non-naturalistic; they are the offspring of
reflective and often romantic moods. The conscious abandonment of naturalism is perhaps symbolized when Schlaf, in visiting the idyllic village
of his birth, remarks that he left Dostoievsky,
Zola, Ibsen, and Tolstoi behind in Berlin. He
revels in the myriad voices of forest solitudes
with the spirit of a Werther, and writes a
series of "prose poems" which interpret the
flowers by his window, lyric in quality, and
through their refrain-like repetitions, almost lyric
in form. Reminiscent, however, of the naturalistic ferment, is the detailed description of a hideous, animalized old woman, lying on a dung-heap,
and perhaps also the questioning reflection on the
act of thinking as possibly a mere chemical process. Yet emphatically a man of his century,
and recognizing its claims, idyllic seclusion cannot
hold Schlaf from the unrest of the great city.

Later stories present problems, sometimes ultra-modern, but, though at times the unlovely, or even the unspeakable, defiles his pages, there is an increasing anti-naturalistic acknowledgment of the unseen and inexplicable sources of life's greatness. As is amply evidenced by the reviews, contemporary criticism perceived in "Papa Hamlet" and in "Neue Gleise" the children of Zola's theories, or at least collateral descendants. It saw also in other novels, some of which were published before the experiments of Holz and Schlaf, a similar relationship to the French naturalist. Some of these novelists, notably Bleibtreu and Conrad, openly acknowledged their discipleship.

Michael Georg Conrad had spent some time in Paris and had made the acquaintance of the great French master; burdened with the responsibility which this involved, he proceeded to interpret Zola's theories to his fellow country-men. In emulative ambition, also, he began a series of ten novels which should comprehend the totality of contemporary life in Munich, a project of which Conrad soon wearied. The material for his stories, the characters and the happenings, Conrad took from the new fields which the naturalists made peculiarly their own; "Was die Isar rauscht" (What the Isar murmurs), for example, the novel with which Conrad opened the series, revels in pollution. A considerable portion of the story centres in a barrack-like tenement, most of whose denizens worry along in the shadows of disrepute and are unabashed. A characteristic stamp is given to this place by one of the occupants who is the editor of an infamous comic journal, called "The Sewer." In ordering the mass of his material, Conrad is annoyingly incoherent and haphazard; to control the material, arranging for proper emphasis and subordination, may have seemed to him like paying a tribute to traditional forms, and hence contrary to the creed of a naturalist. However this may be, in the employment of certain rather discredited methods in narration Conrad has unhesitatingly followed his remote predecessors; he inserts letters such as no human being has written since the days of Clarissa Harlowe, epistles which would cover fifty pages of written manuscript; in reporting conversations, Conrad allows his characters to talk uninterruptedly in alternating periods often a page in length, airing their own and incidentally Conrad's opinions on various timely questions. In these discourses, certainly, the zeal of the propagandist has eaten up the literary convictions of the naturalist.

Through his little volume "Revolution der Literatur," Karl Bleibtreu became a conspicuous figure in the naturalistic movement; it was the clearest call to a new estimate of literary merits, to new methods and new ideals commensurate with contemporary progress and change of thought. In dedicating a book of his own to Conrad, Bleibtreu pays homage to Zola as their master:
"In the name of our master, Nature invites you
        to the feast,

Hats off, and the last bumper to you, Oh, author
    of 'Germinal'! "
But in his own literary work, the predominant
influence of Zola was strikingly transitory. Only
in one book, the collection of short stories entitled "Schlechte Gesellschaft" (Bad Company),
does Bleibtreu swing completely into step with
the other followers of Zola. His long and pon-
derous novel "Grössenwahn" (Megalomania)
was conceived only partly under the spell of naturalism. "Schlechte Gesellschaft" is one of the
most unsavoury books of an unsavoury time. The
lowest type of bar-maid, incipient or full-fledged
harlots, together with the frequenters of the re-
sorts they adorn, constitute the "bad company,"
and they do not belie the designation. The example of Zola seemed to make the choice of such
themes peculiarly commendable in that it emphasized one's emancipation from tradition. Most
of Bleibtreu's work, however, is on another and
higher plane; particularly vivid are his stories
of the Franco-Prussian War, brilliant and start-
lingly realistic, without being a bumptious glorifi-
cation of Prussian victory.

Conrad Alberti was the critic who, perhaps
mindful of a much condemned passage in "La
Terre," asserted that the newer literary æsthetics
recognized no difference between the death of a
great hero and the birth-throes of a cow. Alberti
wrote a series of novels to which he gave the
general title "Der Kampf ums Dasein" (The
Struggle for Existence), the most conspicuous of
which was perhaps the first, "Wer ist der Stär-

kere?" (Who is the Stronger?). The content
was in part what one might expect from the
novelist's principles of selection, but much of the
material was still quite conventional, and the
method decidedly non-experimental.

For the work of Hermann Conradi, another
of the naturalistic group, Zola was also to a large
extent the literary inspiration; Conradi fancied
himself a disciple of Dostoievsky, but his candid
biographers prove that, until Conradi's best-
known work was done, the great Russian novelist was to him a reputation rather than an experience. His "Brutalitäten" displeased even lenient
critics; though he insisted that he cherished only
one intent, to show up life in all its abysmal brutality, the stain upon his literary fame has never
been erased either by his own assertion of innocence nor by the exculpating explanations of his
friends. But Conradi's chief contribution to the
literature of the naturalistic period was the novel
"Adam Mensch." In giving his hero the name
of our first parent and as a surname the German
word which designates a human being, it seems
natural to assume that Conradi essayed to portray the species called "man" through the characterization of a typical specimen, perhaps also
to strip man of his accumulated heritage of accessories, and to reveal him as a primitive being,
— after all, merely a more intelligent animal;
one may remark incidentally that it seems to be
a tactical error to make Adam himself conscious
of the implications of the name he bears. The
philosophy of living which Adam has embraced

appears to be the popular, though incomplete and one-sided, view of Nietzsche's doctrines. And in this, Adam is true to the connotation of his name. The incarnate selfishness of the beast receives the support of an intellectual conviction that each man, as far as his power extends, is warranted or even morally bound to use other men for his own aggrandizement and pleasure. "Brutal ruthlessness" he says "toward others and toward one's own cowardly impulse to spare others,— a feeling which is at bottom affected and arch-egoistic,— is the only principle of progress and development in life." But Adam's tenderer sentiments are not infrequently at odds with his convictions, and he fails to enjoy completely the programme of pleasure, largely at the expense of others, which he assumes to be his right; his pathway is beset with constant annoyances, and one closes the book with the confidence that the approaching marriage, with its signal advance in worldly fortunes, if indeed it really ever takes place, is only a "port of call" and that the troubled soul will soon be on the great deep again. If Conradi proposed to present in Adam Mensch an archetype of human qualities, a typical human being, he certainly confuses his picture in making him the son of an inebriate father and a tuberculous mother. Adam doubtless supplied a problem in heredity such as charmed the early naturalists, but through the possession of interesting though rather irregular antecedents, he would seem to forfeit his position as the "type." However, apart from the implication that Adam is physically and emotionally a pathological specimen, Conradi fails to follow the fascinating leads offered by Adam's inheritance; at any rate the possession of a conscience which unhappily interferes with the pursuit of carnal pleasure is not attributed to weakness inherited from father or mother. Adam's parentage was held out at the beginning of the book as a toothsome morsel for those who at that particular time were delighting in that particular sort of speculation, but in the main, Conradi soon loses sight of it, and devotes his attention to problems in the development of the super-man. An Oriental poet wrote an incomparably sad poem on the joys of living, whether thereby fulfilling or defeating his aim, who shall say? Conradi's intent is not entirely obvious, but apparently in his case also, one may speculate upon the general guidance of the universe and quote the statement of Mephistopheles that he was a part "of that Power which always wills the Bad and always works the Good."

But the somewhat naïve impulse, whether it be due to patriotism or pedagogy, which establishes international cross-references, found the "German Zola" in Max Kretzer. In the early eighties, indeed, many critics did not hesitate to assert that Kretzer was the equal or even the superior of the French giant. In his "Revolution der Literatur," Bleibtreu characterized Kretzer as a "disciple" of Zola but equal to his master. He goes even beyond this in estimating the extent of Kretzer's achievement: "Such power of picturing the soul, such depth in the portrayal of character, such a might of passion, such ruthless energy and audacity in depicting the most fearful misery and sin, such tragic force,— have never been in literature before."

The literature of the new period was essentially urban, because for the time being, the aspects of life which the naturalists selected for special investigation seemed to be primarily of the city; the squalor and low-mindedness of the countryside were discovered later. Thus the immediate critical approval of Kretzer's novels was due in part to his success in reproducing city-backgrounds and to the extraordinary variety and verity of his urban impressions. His popularity with contemporary critics and with the sophisticated reader owed something to a peculiar satisfaction in the nature and the extent of Kretzer's achievement, which neither critic nor reader would have acknowledged. After the founding of the new German Empire, the Germans went about, somewhat naïvely and clumsily, to transform Berlin, their new capital, into a "world-city." What natural development could not do or could do only slowly, the impatient patriots sought to create by fiat. With a self-conscious propaganda, which involves an inherent contradiction, they threw the garments of provincialism ostentatiously aside and covered their nakedness with a cloak of apparent cosmopolitanism. The great world capitals, London and Paris, stood unchallenged as bewildering macrocosms, exhibiting, in all their intensity, the contrasts of modern life. Kretzer seemed to place Berlin by the side of these "world-cities." A world capital must needs be a maelstrom of surging iniquities. Kretzer participated in supplying Berlin with a pleasing consciousness of its own wickedness.

Upon one novel more than any other, "Die Verkommenen" (The Submerged), rests Kretzer's reputation as a German co-worker with Zola. Kretzer takes the fortunes of a family as the theme for his story, and as the current moves forward, really ever downward, irresistibly, fatefully,— the novelist combines with it the slowly moving mass of circumstance which collectively makes up the life of scores of people with whom the individual members of this family come in contact. Around the central theme there is an indefinite fringe for which the author is ever trying to account. Father Merck is an honest workman; he is upright in his obligations, cares little for the ale-house, is industrious and domestic. Though not a paragon of excellences, he is still the type upon which the social fabric rests, the upright man who is willing to work and recognizes his obligations to organized society and to his family. Ida, his wife, is a loyal helpmeet, patient and hard-working. But Merck is out of work; day by day he seeks it, but without avail. Then there is no food and no fire. From their meagre house-furnishings Ida carries one article after another to a conscienceless, cynical pawnbroker and his swindling, smiling wife. Upon the activities of this infamous shop, its keepers and its frequenters, Kretzer expends his finest energies. But the poor must eventually make a decision between a cherished heirloom and a loaf of bread, and the blood-suckers of the poor are ready to assist them in making the decision. The Merck family moves to cheaper quarters, to a gloomy, accursed tenement which is a very charnel-house of woe. Its forty families constitute as many separate exhibits of wretchedness, vice, and degeneracy, streaked here and there with pitiful efforts to effect a release. A larger number of the occupants is made to have "something to do with the story" than might seem natural. But description of life in the mass is a part of Kretzer's technique. A dram-shop in the basement draws the food-money of the starving into its filthy clutches, as if it were established there by some malign power to complete the work of a defective social system. The conception of this dram-shop may owe something to Zola's "L'Assommoir"; it is at any rate a parallel for those who delight in parallels. Merck goes down there "to forget." The baby is accidentally burned to death while Ida and the eldest child, Magda, are out at work, and Merck is sent to prison as an accessory through negligence. After he has served his sentence, desperation lays her hands upon him and he kills a former friend who once lured him to the dram-shop and now taunts him with his fall.

The fortunes of youth in such surroundings are represented primarily by the career of Magda. Hunger forces children into premature toil, and Magda is a brave little worker, selling matches in the restaurants in the evening, though her anxious mother supposes that she is employed in caring for some children. But her pretty face, which grows into real beauty as womanhood steals upon her, is her inevitable undoing. A dishonorable prosperity is hers for a time, until a jealous rival throws vitriol in her face, ruining her beauty; one is reminded of a similar occurrence in Gissing's novel of the London proletariat, "The Nether-World," presumably a chance resemblance. Deserted by her companion, Magda sends her baby home to her mother, and then after an unavailing struggle to earn her daily bread, she ends her life in company with her real lover, a young man of talent whose efforts to rise above his class have collapsed into hopelessness. These are the main narrative threads of "Die Verkommenen," but there is in reality a tangled skein of characters and happenings; with each family in the tenement a corresponding set of employers is provided, all equally alluring to the novelist and leading into a labyrinth of interesting but comparatively unrelated pathways, save as the author, perhaps ignoring the probabilities, provides a pattern of coincidental connections.

The year previous to the appearance of "Die Verkommenen," Kretzer published his first important novel, "Die Betrogenen" (The Deceived), distinctly inferior to "Die Verkommenen," but something more than a mere promise of sincere and vigorous work. "Die Betrogenen" are working girls. In the main Kretzer does not sentimentalize their lot, nor seek excuses for their

lapses, still less does he sink into heroics in depicting their struggle against the stream, but with
sympathy for the weak, for those who have never
really had a chance, he shows how native characteristics yield sooner or later to the influence of a
degrading *milieu,* which indeed begins its insidious
process of pollution even before the first letters
are learned.

"Die Verkommenen" and "Die Betrogenen"
contain, doubtless, an indirect indictment of the
social order, but the charge is a general one,
sweeping and inclusive, though confused by the
very multitude and variety of concrete examples
of social injustice. The student of social problems might draw, as from life itself, material for
a dozen separate theses, but Kretzer himself does
not select a single problem or a related group of
problems for his consideration. The problems
are inherent, inferable, but are not stated as such.
Kretzer is in this the more perfect naturalist. In
"Die Bergpredigt" (The Sermon on the Mount)
and "Meister Timpe" the novelist concentrates
on certain phases of the great blunder called organized society, and the novels themselves gain
in definition.

"Die Bergpredigt" tries to uncover the crumb-
ling feet of clay on which religious orthodoxy
stands. A church which was founded in divine
compassion is a whited sepulchre of hypocrisy,
while the poor are dying at her gates. In "Meister Timpe," Kretzer presents the transitional
period when machinery was replacing the skill of
human hands, a theme beloved of the story-teller

since the days of Charlotte Brontë's "Shirley."
He incorporates the tragedy of this change in the
person of his hero who can not realize that his
antiquated notions are incompatible with progress.
Meister Timpe takes an honorable place beside
the stubborn, honest old man,— Hoffmann's
Meister Martin, Hebbel's Meister Anton, Ludwig's Erbförster,—whose obstinacy and whose
pride of profession have added strength, and humour, and pathos to the pages of the German
drama and novel. He is the embodiment of the
old school of honest industry and solid workmanship; in his shop, too, the kindly old relationships,
patriarchal perhaps, between master and workmen, built on mutual regard and on pride in
honest work, have not been standardized or me-
chanized by social democracy. But all this is
gradually undermined through the new fashion
of work and the new generation of workers. A
factory is built in the neighbourhood with which
the workshop can not compete. And the old man,
leaving the silent shop, treads the streets of
Berlin in pursuit of employment. Social democracy of the most scarlet variety then adds
the old man to her ranks, though he had once
abhorred her very name, and gains in him a
violent agitator to class warfare. Finally the
old man perishes in the cellar of his own house,
where he has barricaded himself against the
officers of the law. The bitterness of his
cup has been made more bitter through the
defection of his only son; this is the hapless repro-
bate Franz, a conventional and rather unconvinc-

ing specimen of the unrepentant prodigal, a
naughty, spoiled child, who spurns the simple
homeliness of his youthful environment, and goes
over actively to the enemy. "Meister Timpe" is
Kretzer's most consistent and moving novel, and
its hero his most living and memorable character.
The critics found and still find in "Meister
Timpe" an arresting resemblance to Zola's "Au
Bonheur des Dames." The resemblance lies obviously in the general problem of the relationship
of individual labour, operating as a unit, to the
organized activity of the many; a large manu-
facturing or mercantile establishment, working on
a large scale and with all modern facilities, crush-
es its old-fashioned and unprogressive competitors. But while Zola, soon after the beginning of
his story, establishes the centre of interest in the
relentless activities of the great "department
store," its inner life and the relations of its scores
of employees, Kretzer maintains the focus of his
attention in Timpe's workshop. Banaus, Zola's
umbrella merchant, whose trade diminishes, who
even turns to mending umbrellas himself, when
the last of his employees has gone, or old Baudu,
the proprietor of a drapery establishment, whose
business is undermined by the success of the gilded
"emporium" across the way, are somewhat pallid
minor personages; Meister Timpe remains the
protagonist, a figure of almost tragic grandeur.
Some elements of Kretzer's plot are doubtless
conventional, unreal, and theatrical; material is
obviously invented or manipulated for emotional
effect, and scientific principles are forgotten in

melodramatic success; but in this respect there is
nothing in Kretzer's story which violates the basic
principles of naturalism so completely as the mix-
ture of "Pamela" and "Cinderella" which actually
forms the main plot of Zola's novel.

The sordid dulness of naturalistic themes
brought an inevitable reaction. Zola himself re-
lieved the heaviness of his Rougon-Marquart series through an appeal to the immaterial world in
"Le Rêve," and Hauptmann in Germany placed
the vision world of "Hanneles Himmelfahrt"
(The Assumption of Hannele) beside the unspeakable meanness and depravity of "Vor Son-
nenaufgang" (Before Dawn). Kretzer's novel
"Das Gesicht Christi" (The Vision of Christ)
serves similarly as a foil to the desolation of "Die
Verkommenen." Hauptmann projects the fevered
visions of a dying girl against the misery of a
country alms-house, and challenges our learning
to find a purely natural explanation. Kretzer
places his visions quite beyond the reach of psychological analysis;— they cannot be explained
away. The central scene of the story is a wretched room where a working-man and his whole family exist. The father has no work, and there is
no money to buy food. But the worker has
nevertheless not lost faith in the reality of Divine
Providence. In the ugly tenement he tries to
protect his children from the evil which surrounds
them and lures them, and to establish and preserve a sense of honour and decency. The action
of the story occupies but little more than a single
day. In the evening, the haggard, hungry man

goes out in search of something to eat, and two of the children go with him. The baby dies during their absence, virtually starved. And the following day, Easter Sunday, is filled with the father's effort to obtain honourable burial for the little child. But this is only half of the story, this pitiless uncovering of human woe. As Andorf and his hungry children walk through the streets, looking in at lighted windows and jostled by a holiday throng, they see the form of Christ walking among men. In that alley tenement of wretchedness and vice, Andorf knocks on a neighbour's door, seeking temporary aid; the neighbour glances back at the door from which the disheartened father has retreated, and sees the figure of Christ standing where he had stood. So, too, on the awful day of seeking, Andorf visits the officer of the poor, who is vexed at such an intrusion in the midst of his holiday pleasure. But when he looks back into the office, where he had grudgingly granted an interview, he sees the form of Christ sitting where the visitor had sat. And when Andorf trundles the coffin out to the cemetery on a wheelbarrow, while Easter crowds fill the streets, thousands see the figure of Christ walking behind him.

In "Das Gesicht Christi," it seems quite obvious, there can be no question of applying the methods of research in the psychological laboratory; the supernatural cannot be interpreted "naturally," as pure hallucination. We are confronted with an intentional use of symbol. The striking contradiction between intensified earthly misery and the dimly recognized proximity of divine power may appear to the critic as fantastic, as a cheap method of producing high lights, perhaps of gaining for the sympathetic reader a comfortable sense of ultimate justice, akin to the sentimental view of the last judgment as a mere re-distribution of rewards. But Kretzer's purpose seems clear. He presents in bodily form the higher vision which envelops us; by the presence of the benign figure, seen at times but indubitably ever-present, he seeks not merely a colourful contrast but symbolizes the unbroken contact between his hero's faith and its object. That other people and not Andorf himself see the vision is apparently an intentional tribute to the vigour of Andorf's faith, which does not waver, however great the trials to which it is subjected, while the vision appears as a rebuke to the faithless. The novel may perhaps be the elaboration of an idea derived from Tolstoi's story of Martin the Cobbler, "Where Love is, there God is"; but, be that as it may, Kretzer's story is an effective and touching presentation of the eternal hope.

Despite the accuracy of Kretzer's observations, despite the compelling power of individual situations which he has created, his novels fall short of real greatness when tested by the highest standards, indeed when compared with the work of the great French master. Kretzer's more noteworthy novels, even those upon which his reputation rests, are deficient in structural organization. In no one of them, with the possible exception of "Meister Timpe," does a central situation move forward in clear progressive steps and without cumbersome irrelevancies, to an inevitable conclusion. In some of the minor novels, to be sure, a consistent, well-rounded story is told, but it is of the conventional, lending library type of fiction, in which ends are attained through a transparent manœuvering of the material; but these stories are almost negligible quantities in estimating the position of Kretzer as a novelist. The creative imagination is with Kretzer awkward and shortsighted. He cannot achieve a design of grand dimensions, for he sees only a few things at a time, albeit with extraordinary exactness; within a restricted range his presentment of truth is unimpeachable, but when he looks up to get the broader view, he is bothered and bewildered by the multiplicity of his impressions; the world is too much with him. His best work is a kind of mosaic without unity of plan or grandeur of design. Bit by bit he arranges his pieces, and some of the individual mosaics are of unsurpassed workmanship.

Then, too, in the more noteworthy novels, one is seized by the suspicion, which will not down, that Kretzer so manages his material, through accumulations, as to produce the greatest possible sum total of anguish concentrated in a given space. A resentment haunts us that the novelist sets out to shock the indifferent into attention, to overwhelm us with the extremities of a class whose cause he has espoused. In so far as this suspicion has foundation then, his work becomes tainted with propaganda, and he ceases to be a naturalist.

That truth is stranger than fiction is an adage
behind which the naturalistic novelist must not
seek refuge; the unusual and the unexpected must
not happen in his pages. Kretzer makes over-
abundant use of tense and arresting contrasts,
he splashes his canvas with melodramatic colours.
Not infrequently, for example, he manœuvers his
characters in such a way as to provide for coincidental meetings, fraught indeed with emotional
appeal but smacking of cheaper fiction. In "Drei
Weiber" (Three Women), Paulus is a musician
of unusual gifts, worthy of a nation's interest, but
poverty compels him to earn his daily bread in a
very humble exercise of his musicianship. One
night, as he plays in a dance-hall of ill repute, he
encounters the girl whose love had once been more
than life to him. In the days of her discreditable
prosperity, Magda in "Die Verkommenen" sees
her father, worn with hunger and disgrace, selling
little toys which he has whittled from bits of
wood; she commands her rich lover, as she stands
in the shadow, to buy one of these at double the
price. This latter motive is, oddly enough, repeated in Clara Viebig's "Das tägliche Brot"
(Our Daily Bread). Robert Seidel, the hero of
"Die Betrogenen," is witness of the suicide of a
working-girl, who, crazed by hunger and fruitless
effort to support her child, has fallen into the
mire of sin; among the women who gather about,
peering into the dark waters, Robert finds his own
lost sister.

The working classes and particularly the lower
levels of the bourgeoisie are rich in humorous

types and so-called "originals." Kretzer is fond
of relieving the squalor and unloveliness of his
underworld by the insertion of humorous genre
pictures, which may or may not have anything to
do with the story in the narrower sense. In this
phase of his work, both as to matter and manner,
Kretzer touches Dickens rather than Zola; particularly in his pictures of social events among the
proletarians, whether the background be purely
domestic or publicly convivial, Kretzer is unmistakably the pupil of Dickens. He himself confesses the source of his inspiration. In the otherwise inconspicuous novel "Waldemar Tempel,"
there is a group of characters distinctly of the
Dickens stamp, and a series of meetings among
them might fit quite neatly into a story by the
English novelist. The hero, an irresponsible
cavalier and "man about town," is left penniless
by the death of his father, and at the same time
through the will of an eccentric uncle, he is to
receive a substantial property on condition that
he earn his own living for a year. Waldemar's
experiences in the fulfillment of this scheme, his
humorous efforts at concealment, the love of work
for its own sake which gradually masters him,
and his respect for his fellow-workers, form the
substance of the book, and display the "tendenz"
of its author. But distinctly more successful in
workmanship and in verity, are the struggles of
the other relatives, the presumptive heirs, headed
by a soap-dealer, to frustrate Waldemar's endeavours. These greedy spirits are humorously

middle-class, and Kretzer revels in their narrow and acrid Philistinism.

The collection of Samaritans gathered at the pastor's house in "Die Bergpredigt" is a further case in point. Kretzer prolongs the scene far beyond its merits as a link in the plot, because he is amused at the characters of his own creation, such as the woman who, in a species of antiphonal refrain, attributes all social evils to the celibacy of the clergy, and the "original" whose association with ecclesiastical benevolence is due to his interest in the sale of communion wines. The hideous environment out of which the heroine of the same novel is snatched, Kretzer manages to enliven through the picturesque presence of her step-father; the latter is evidently a relative of Mr. Micawber, though much lower in the social scale and indulging with a really conscious abandon in the determination to reap all possible benefits from calculated sloth. But he is cruel and brutal; in these aspects of his character perhaps he bears more than a mere family resemblance to M. Lantier in Zola's "L'Assommoir." The humorous vagaries of ale-house keepers and the eccentricities of their guests, Kretzer has at his finger-tips, as is attested in one novel after another, and in scenes which frequently stand outside of the story. Here Kretzer appears as a humorist, and his humour is distinctly of the Dickens sort, mainly achieved through exaggerated emphasis on characteristic traits. Dickens began his career as the author of humorous sketches, amazing in their vigour and verisimilitude, but verging into caricature.

He learned to patch these pieces together into a fairly consistent whole, and became a novelist, but, though he notes accurately the just proportions of his larger design, the lure of the sketchable in character and incident often leads to irrelevant inclusions. The same is true of Kretzer, though he often loses the design altogether in the fascination of the detail.

Kretzer also stands beside Dickens in his undisguised sympathy with human suffering and his indignation at apathetic onlookers. He neither observes nor records with scientific impartiality. More than one German critic declared Kretzer superior to Zola because he did not exclude or try to exclude his own "heart" from a participation in his imagined but still vividly realized world,— which, one must admit, begs the question of naturalism completely. Indeed, Bleibtreu apparently held the opinion that the acceptance of naturalism in its strictest interpretation was frankly impossible for a German author, save perhaps in isolated products, which are mere *tours de force,* unnatural and essentially exotic. The German spirit is, according to this critic, lyrical and philosophical in its native endowment; the German demands both a soaring above the material world and a deepening of the emotional life. One might grant the presence of a lyric note in the German make-up,— it is often called perhaps by other names,— which requires of literature a more frank emotional appeal. But all literature, in so far as it has been worthy of the name, has been "a soaring above the material world," has been this and nothing but this. If literary work thus characterized and thus stimulated is irreconcilible with naturalism, then naturalism has no place in our counsels. If we had no other basis for our conclusions, the course of the naturalistic movement itself demonstrates clearly enough that any effort to record in literature one's observations of the phenomena of that part of nature which we call human life is "unnatural" and futile, if it is not at the same time "a soaring above the material world." The nature of man is to think in terms of an immaterial world.

Arno Holz, as theorist of German naturalism, explained the on-coming of the naturalistic movement as the result of an inevitable law or tendency, inherent in the nature of things: "Art tends to be, or rather to become nature again," he said, implying that in some way art ceases to be nature, having once been identical with it, and then through the operation of his law, inevitably tends to resume this identity. This particular sentence, together with certain amplifying phrases which followed it, attained great fame as a new statement of important truth. As a matter of fact, if one can turn a neat new phrase which touches the age-old antithesis between art and nature, a train of disciples is assured. Holz's dictum has enough of suggestion to arrest and perhaps to deceive, but on reflection one perceives its vacuity; it is either meaningless or false. To insist that art and nature are or can become identical is to maintain a contradiction in terms. Art is, in its essence, not nature but a use of nature, its process is the manipulation of certain phenomena, the arrangement of a new pattern, consisting of selected and re-arranged elements. Art presents and represents nature; and a return to nature which has any foundation in reality is nothing more or less, despite the recurrent enthusiasms of the centuries, than a renewed insistence on a direct and accurate observation of the phenomena of nature in place of an indirect transcription from the observations of others. If nature is the well-spring of inspiration, the waters become stale and insipid, when retained too long and carried too far from their source. The artist must return to the fountain, and must not expect other artists to supply him from their pitchers. Naturalism, so far as it did literature a service and not a dis-service was merely a vigorous call to precisely this kind of return to nature.

And naturalism, in spite of its exaggerations and distortions, wrought in this way inestimable good. Imitating the natural scientists, the new men of letters sought truth through the observation of phenomena, and for this purpose they necessarily sharpened the eye and ear for the accurate recording of things seen and heard, even for things seen and heard only by the eye and ear of the imagination. They acquired patience and industry in the observation of character and conduct, in the accumulation of facts and realities which might be used in creating new realities; they gained a new and acute perception of the inevitable relation between past and present, whether or not it was frankly expressed in scientific terms of heredity and environment. In this way they demonstrated that the attitude of scientific research is appropriate even in those who present only imagined segments of life; they insisted, and with right, that literature, in recording the adventures of our generation in the world of the spirit, should take into account whatever of value had been won through diligent inquiry into the phenomena of material things. We may pardon the vagaries and excesses of the scientific novelist if by example and precept he has enriched our experience and has trained men to seek the truth with unprejudiced eyes.

RICARDA HUCH THE MODERN RO-MANTICIST

THE naturalists were so intent upon accumulating the details of life, so absorbed in
recording the particles and atoms, that they often
failed to perceive their collective significance.
They were like a man who stands too near to
a curtain of some strange and cunning weave
which, from a certain distance, shows a pattern
of iridescent and everchanging splendour. But,
even in the days of sober scrutiny, there have
been those who have insisted that the things of
life, in their multiplicity, triviality, and evanes-
cence, may have more than a surface value, more
than a purely perceptive meaning. There have
been those who do not give up the hope, and
with the hope, the task, of essaying an interpretation. They seek a vantage-point of observation;
they do not stand too close to life, but in a kind
of reflective aloofness, they trace the lines of
its symmetry. Such a one is Ricarda Huch.

With the exception of a few *Novellen*, to be
sure, Ricarda Huch has devoted herself for
more than a decade to a kind of historical story-
telling, to works which, strictly speaking, are
neither histories nor novels. One can appreciate
her delight in the "stranger fiction" of Italy's
story in the nineteenth century, or the zest with
which she seeks to grasp and realize the tragedy
of the Thirty Years' War; there were giants in
those days, and not of the nursery variety. The

imagined material with which she adorns the record of historical fact and fills its interstices raises history to a higher power of intelligibility and force. Reality becomes more real. But in all this she is, as it were, only the artist's assistant when she might be the designer of the whole; to create the mere by-work of history, however illuminating, seems unworthy of her singular creative gifts. Her position in German literature will, it would seem, be determined primarily upon the basis of her four earlier novels which were published between 1893 and 1904.

Ricarda Huch's first novel "Erinnerungen von Ludolf Ursleu dem Jüngeren" is in craftsmanship the most perfect achievement of her story-telling. As a monk in a Swiss cloister Ludolf Ursleu looks back over the experiences of his life and records them. It is, as its title suggests, a book of remembrance, and its manifold substance is welded into unity by the dominating presence of a retrospective mood. The novelist never forgets the monk's hand which guides her pen nor the mellowing distance from which the events are seen.

Ludolf Ursleu is the son of a prosperous merchant in a North German Hansa town, unmistakably Hamburg. The family leads a life of cultivated elegance; "it was looked upon in our house as the real task of man to wear life as a beautiful garment or jewel" is Ludolf's way of stating it, and more than once he compares their manner of living to that of the Phæacians whom Ulysses describes as emulating the life of the Gods. Ludolf has a younger sister Galeida, of a winning comeliness and an inexplicable, almost mystic fascination. In her character, strangely contradictory, self-willed and mysteriously will-less, lies the tragedy of the household. From French Switzerland comes Lucile to be a kind of governess and companion to Galeida, and she marries Ezard, Ludolf's cousin. Ezard is the son of Uncle Harre, a local physician of scholarly distinction. The unseen forces seemingly had conspired together to fashion Ezard Ursleu for a king among men, so beautiful, so strong, so god-like was he. But some malignant counter-force enters in and distorts the perfect design; a black line is drawn through its former symmetry, and it is thrown into the waste-basket.

All too late the mistake of this marriage is seen. For, as the great-grandfather had long insisted, destiny had intended Ezard and Galeida for one another. The character of the great-grandfather is, by the way, interestingly and pitifully woven into the fabric of the story; he is not a participant in the action, only an observer of the collapse of all he loves. The passion of the two young lovers, Ezard and Galeida, is irresistible and all-consuming; once developed, it becomes like a demoniac possession. It is as though they had partaken of a magic love philtre; they are no more able to resist this enchantment than were Tristan and Isolde. On this passion the family goes to ruin; it is the canker which eats the life out of happiness and fortune. The mother fades away in her beauty and dies, the

father loses heart and then takes his own life;
the business house of the Ursleus totters and
falls. Yet nothing can alter it. Whether Ezard
and Galeida meet, or, listening for a time to the
despairing appeals of the family, avoid one
another,— it is still the same. Galeida goes
away to a conservatory of music to perfect her
signal talents in music and becomes a concert
violinist of renown. But the elemental passion is
unchanged.

Then comes the tragedy of tragedies. The
cholera sweeps through the city. A weird prophetic dream haunts Ludolf at the rumour of the
first case; the figure of the pestilence is different,
but the horror of the dream-symbolism reminds
one of the awful terror of Böcklin's "Pest." The
ghoulish spirit wanders everywhere through the
city, summoning high and low. Love of life and
love of beauty make feverish efforts to rescue a
scanty dole of hours for joy, and to present a
steely front to grief and fear. But to forget or ignore Death whilst he stalks the earth is perhaps
more than even Florentine story-tellers could ac-
complish. Lucile dies of the pestilence, following
the death of her eldest child. The mystery of her
death casts on Ezard the shadow of guilt; it happened not contrary to his will. With the death of
Lucile the story takes a further step into the
inscrutable realm of destiny. Galeida goes to
Switzerland to accommpany Ezard thither with
the body of Lucile. There she falls under the
spell of Gaspard, Lucile's younger brother, who,
though monosyllabic and uncouth, exercises over

her a kind of mesmeric, hypnotic power. The
love which has consumed all, which has been co-
extensive with living, is now swallowed up in a
new passion. Ezard stands aghast at the miracle,
and Galeida becomes a mysterious terror to herself. Her august will is powerless but to do
Gaspard's, and finally she commits suicide at the
command of his imperious and capricious fancy.
Ezard lives on for a time, a money-getter, lost in
mercantile projects; the ideals of life are dead.
Fate has had its way with the Ursleus; but it
has spared little Harre, the son of Ezard and
Lucile. Perhaps the tragic potentialities of the
Ursleus have now become exhausted, and the
little boy will be left in peace.

Despite the simplicity of plot, essentially the
familiar stage triangle or rather, one such triangle strangely shifting into another, we perceive
not only that the happenings of which it is composed are exceptional, but that the sequence of
events has, particularly at the determinative
points, little foundation in normal reality. To
assure a coherence of structure, to replace the
expected congruence between normal character
and normal deeds, a powerful and pervasive sense
of inevitability is secured. Indeed through the
method of narration, a conception of fate, really
Greek in its intensity, dominates the book; it is
the merciless logic of retrospect. Ludolf records
the events; because they *were,* he refuses to believe that they could have been otherwise. As
the Greeks in their theatres were always keenly
sensible of the onward sweep of the tragedy, in

no way deceived by the illusory moments of re-
tarded action, because they knew the end from
the beginning, so here the perception of tragic
inevitability is communicated.

And under the monk's cowl, Ludolf preserves
an attitude toward life and death which is pagan
and Greek, and not Christian. Not the will to
draw near to God but a total distrust of life has
brought this son of North German Protestantism
to his solitary cell; "There is nothing in life,
absolutely nothing which has permanence . . . .
Life is a bottomless, shoreless sea," he exclaims
at the beginning of the book, and "Be still, my
soul, it is past!" are the words of resignation
which close it. However often the rosary may
pass through his hands and his lips mumble
prayers, his mind is held by a love of vanished
beauty and a passion for the life behind him,
which is Hellenic, at the other pole of thought
from the ascetic ideal to which he outwardly
bows. Ludolf clings to his world of earthly
memories; his days are not spent in confident and
joyful expectation of a world of reunion and
reconciliation for which this world of blighted
beauty is but an unworthy ante-chamber. His
posture is, once again, Hellenic,— is that so
touchingly portrayed on Attic gravestones, a
folding of hands in mute resignation, with faces
turned toward what has been rather than toward
what may be.

For her second novel Ricarda Huch took her
material from a very different sphere. Narrow,
winding streets lead from modern, mercantile

Trieste up to the heights where the old cathedral
stands; a network of alleys and court-yards, ill-
paved and malodorous, covers the steep hillside.
The houses seem to struggle wearily upwards, to
peer over one another at the blue glory of the
Adriatic which stretches below. In the midst of
this hill-side city stands a diminutive Roman
triumphal arch. It is merely mentioned in Baede-
ker, and the chance traveller has no means of
discovering whose now forgotten victories it once
immortalized. One side of the arch is built into
the wall of a tenement. Grass grows over the
top of it. It was perhaps the contrast between
this pompous monument of antiquity and the
squalor of its present surroundings which suggested to Ricarda Huch the theme of "Aus der
Triumphgasse."

At first perhaps the story seems rather a series
of sketches out of "Triumph Alley" than a novel
in the more rigid sense of the word. But, as one
discovers on closer inspection, the work has true
unity and a genuine consecutiveness of narration.
At the centre of the narrative stand a poor old
woman called Farfalla, and her cripple boy
Riccardo. To call Farfalla old is indeed false to
the mere record of the years, but youth and age
stand side by side in Triumph Alley, there is no
middle ground. The maidens display an opulent
beauty, but youth yields soon to wrinkled, colour-
less, and leaden-footed age. Years before the
beginning of the story Farfalla had been deserted
by her worthless, tavern-haunting husband. She
has battled importunately with adversity and has

forced from cruel circumstance a niggardly existence for herself and her seven children. By the
sweat of her brow and the sleeplessness of her
nights they have been fed and clothed. She is
too proud to beg,— except for flowers. One can
see in the clear, quiet depths of her eyes an ever
suppressed and never satisfied hunger for sleep
and tears. Yet even in life's bitterness Farfalla
preserves a kind of detachment; — a discriminat-
ing balance, a philosophic humour, cruel at times
and cynical, lift her out of her class. Riccardo,
a cripple from babyhood, is half child and half
man, wasting away in inexpressible pain. Though
he is querulous and exacting, especially toward
his mother, Riccardo's couch is a centre of light
and joy. There is good cheer wherever one hears
the click of his crutch; the people of the alley
gather in the evening by the fountain to listen to
his harmonica, or to laugh at what seems to them
the drollness of his imaginings. Riccardo has a
poet's soul; he is a dreamer of dreams, although,
or perhaps because, he is already consciously
looking into an open grave.

The varied life of Triumph Alley pulses about
these two. It is the story of those whose lives
are begun in wretchedness, whose days are spent
in withering poverty and often in brutal crime.
They drag after them a weight of hunger and of
shame. Sometimes there is work, but often not,
and then the men hesitate to come home to hungry
children, and the women play lotto by the fountain
to forget that there is no bread at home. Feverish
is the sometime gaiety, the merriment of the

dance and the lust of wine, until one awakes suddenly to the gray living under the blue sky.

And yet, pitifully enough, these people have not all lost the human heritage of hope; happiness with fortune seems still among life's possibilities. Much is expected from the return of absent ones. They are mostly runaways, departed under a cloud of delinquency, shiftlessness, or cowardice. And they return usually as prodigals for whom no feast is spread. The people of the Alley are "orphan children," or perhaps, "step-children" of religious faith. They do not believe that God loves the poor; they jest about the Virgin's method of answering their prayers. But, as Farfalla explains, in misery they stretch out their arms to Heaven, "just on a chance," even as the drowning man cries for help, though he knows there is no one far and wide who can hear him. So they go yearly on a pilgrimage to a distant shrine,—half a dimly remembered devotion, half a vague superstition; nothing will be lost, it is at any rate a day's outing, and there is a faint gambling chance that after all something might be gained. It is a varied assortment of woes which they bring to the shrine; one mother prays for the death of her unborn child, and weary Farfalla for the death of her best-loved son. For life had become a torture to her, lest she should die first, and there be no one to care for him. Death indeed is spoken of very freely in the Alley. People wait with waggish jests for one another to die, for only a limited number of begging licenses is allowed.

Riccardo and a wavering consumptive even wager as to which shall go first.

Man is a primitive beast in Triumph Alley. Murder after murder stains the pages of the story, culminating in Pasquale's fiendish slaying of his own child in order to torture his wife. Weakness and frivolity prevail often where violent passions do not control; poor little foolish Anetta makes ill return for the help given her; "she would still be the same if you were to set her on a king's throne . . . she would throw her crown in the mire and go to ruin."

Is it a savage irony that those of Farfalla's kin for whom the future seems to hold the most in store arc Carmelo, her son, who is a murderer in the work-house and his wife Galanta who has been a woman of the streets? That even Antoinetta, the "laughing dove" who has kept herself undefiled, gives herself in despair at life's contradictions to the most bestial of the Alley beasts, then curses life and dies? Is Farfalla's life a hideous tragi-comedy that her efforts to rear her children to honesty and usefulness seem so woefully wrecked, that she works on with withered hands to keep that son alive the very continuance of whose life she most fears? Even when he is gone, she buys oil to keep a light burning for him because he loved it, rather than buy bread for herself. The habit of self-sacrifice has become too strong to break. Dimly perhaps one catches the symbolism of "Triumph Alley"; it is not written in hopeless irony, the splendour of the past contrasted with the ignominy of the pres-

ent; it is the story of an heroic soul. Through
the triumphal arch the conquerors walk, not
merely a chained and desperate train of captives.

Contradictory as it may seem in view of its
darker, sordid substance, the story is shot through
with romantic suggestion. The narrator is simply
the chance owner of a house in the Alley, chance
brings him there and the fascination of its little
world holds him in thrall. About the sordid and
the mean he spreads his veil of romance; through
his reflections the dream world touches the real
world. Reality is often tawdry, brutal, and
loathsome, but much lies outside material realities, and on this our attention is fixed. Round
about the stories of Triumph Alley the faint outlines of another story lie, as a kind of frame. It
is unobtrusive, but after all it is a part of the
picture as a frame should be. The narrator allows
us glimpses now and then of the life he leads in
his own world, and of Lisabella, the woman whom
he loves. His experiences in the Alley, even as
an interested observer, occasionally and capriciously yielding to benevolent impulses, react upon
his life in his own sphere. They force upon him
the riddle of life, and afford at the same time a
dim apprehension of its answer; they convince
him of the unity of human life, however hidden
or distorted, they smother in him the complacent
satisfaction in the possession of individual happiness. "I do not know why I do not throw
myself in your arms," he says to Lisabella at
the end, "why I must weep when I think of you."
The device of a narrator who, to use the figure

suggested above, is not in the picture but still belongs to it, is a peculiarly happy one when used expertly.

The next story also bears a symbolic title "Vita Somnium Breve," and the novelist enforced the significance of her choice by inserting as a frontispiece Böcklin's allegorical picture bearing that name. In the foreground beside a tiny stream two babies sit on a daisy-starred greensward; one of them watches a flower, which he has just launched, float away on the surface of the water. In the background is a marble fountain, the source of the rill; it bears the legend *Vita Somnium Breve*. Before it stands a woman in the full glory of womanhood; beyond a warrior rides away. But, above a greybeard sits, looking vacantly into space. Death stands behind him with arms uplifted for the final blow. In later editions the title of this novel has been changed to "Michael Unger."

"So this is life!" exclaims Michael Unger in the first words of the book. Day by day he goes to business; it is simply a glorified version of the peasant's round, carrying one's sacks to the mill, year in, year out. Wealth and social position are his; he has a handsome wife and a child of beauty and promise. Yet how is he distancing his father, who has also gained great possessions, who has a beautiful wife and sons to bear his hopes? About the old mansion of the family stood rustling poplars whose song Michael had interpreted in his boyhood to mean "Oh, Life! Oh, Beauty!" These words form a kind of "leitmotiv" for the story, recurring again and again. Has he advanced toward a realization of his dream of life? And whither has the beauty fled? Into his life now comes Rosa Sarthorn, comes to paint the portrait of Mario, the little boy. She is "the gold-ground of an every-day picture," her eyes are like a magic fountain in which the beauty and the wonder of the world are mirrored; she is the child of Mother Earth, and to Mother Earth her prayers are said. Dissatisfied with a meaningless parting from Rosa, when her task is done, Michael follows her, hardly realizing the nature of his own action, obeying an irresistible power within him. A scene of lover's rapture follows, a transfusion of two souls, as by some magic power made one. The rescue of himself from conventional and petrifying activity, the development of his capacities into a realization of his full self, now become a resolve. He decides to live his own life in spite of traditional responsibilities, to defy the conventionalizing current which has hitherto borne him along. As the boat takes him from Rosa's side across the lake, he stands at the prow and hears amid the stormy waves the old melody of the poplars, "Oh, Life! Oh, Beauty!" It is not too late for the realization of the dream. His father greets his request for release from the firm with incredulous scorn, but Michael craftily uses the matrimonial plans of his younger brother and induces him to give up his career as an artist and to enter the business in his place. Michael is free.

The first step toward fulfillment is a period
of residence at a university. The new environment confirms Michael in the wisdom of his
decision. The men and women of his new circle
are younger than he, so he lives in an atmosphere
of their untried enthusiasms. He is borne on
by their very zest in living as a purely physical
experience. These youths look with a healthy
scepticism upon the heritage of the ages; it is
all theirs for the asking, but they are conscious
of their rights to question its value, as of their
destiny to add to it. The women of the group,
newly admitted to university life as a school of
directed and purposeful enthusiasms, surrender
more completely than the men to the lure of the
radical, to the fascination of demolition. They
are possessed by a longing for that which they
can not name or describe. Much of the vague
iconoclasm in their dreaming derives from the
interesting personality of the baron, a professor
in the university. His intellect commands respect,
and his character wins affection; to one of the
women the baron is "her idea of God"— "I am
only a flame of worship," she says, "an eternal
lamp which no priestess needs to feed or watch."
Both young men and young women are inflamed
by an emotional intoxication which is clearly
assigned in part to the unwonted nature of their
companionship. They exult in the glorious assurance that life lies before them, all untouched,
incomparably beautiful and new. Michael is led
by their fellowship to think himself justified in

ignoring that irrevocable part of his own life
which he has already trod.

These university years are interrupted by
vacation days with Rosa, and obligatory visits to
his home. His wife, Verena, absolutely refuses
to consent to a separation, and remains obdurate
as the years pass. She grows in strength of
character and in self-control; with the gradual
death of her love for him, which was almost worship, she ceases to look on him as master; she
outmatches him in argument, and her unperturbed
composure, her reflective coolness, irritate him
to unmanning passion. He is angry and disheartened at his debasement in his own eyes; he
is not accustomed to be the seeker, nor to have
his purposes questioned. His parents look on
him with mortification and indignant scorn when,
after several years, they learn the underlying
cause of his defection. The younger brother
Raphael, weak and worthless as he is, twits
Michael with the life he leads. To Michael the
relationship to Rosa is something unutterably
holy, and with amazed resentment he sees that
others understand it in the light of an ordinary
liaison.

Michael does not spend these years at the
university in vain. He achieves a real success as
a scholar, conducts biological investigations on
the Adriatic shore, is then entrusted with the
care of a biological station on the Mediterranean,
and finally is offered a promising position as
leader of scientific work on the Amazon. The
crisis comes. Michael determines at last to defy

convention and take Rosa with him. Now the
very summit of his years seems reached; for
Verena now acquiesces in his wishes for a divorce.
But Michael cannot take little Mario with him;
he parts from the boy as if for a brief time, and
goes to Rosa. But in the midst of the joy of
attainment, the father is tortured by the thought
of Mario's face when he shall learn the truth
about his father's leave-taking,— the little boy
who trusted in him. He breaks with Rosa and
goes back to his child. In the old home matters
have become continually worse. Michael's father
has lost his grip on the business, debts accumulate,
and complete disaster is imminent. The old man
takes his own life. Michael goes back and puts
his shoulder to the wheel. He returns to the
activity which he has spurned, to the humdrum
family life with the wife he has forsaken. Mario
grows toward manhood, begins to lead a life of
his own, and to insist upon it, even as his father
had done. His ambitious dreams torment his
sobered father, who cannot convince him of their
substancelessness. And so it goes on in one
eternal round. Michael has returned to all
against which he rebelled; he has lost the fruit
of devoted years, the supreme passion of life is
dead, even the boy for whom the surrender was
made, now lives a life of callous indifference,
ignorant of his father's sacrifice. Rosa too, after
her marriage with the baron, descends to staid
domesticity; the problems of kitchen and nursery
upon a rather insecure financial foundation, replace the insurgent dreams of youth.

This seems like a very un-romantic ending for a story which is surcharged with romantic feeling. The romanticists condemned the ending of Goethe's "Wilhelm Meister" as prosaic; the words of Friedrich which stand at the end of the novel seemed to them like irony: "You seem to me like Saul, the son of Kish, who set out to seek for his father's asses and found a kingdom," for Wilhelm's kingdom seemed too distinctly of this world. Ricarda Huch, it would seem, is on Goethe's side, though she takes a very romantic way of arriving there. The controlling force in all action is emotion. The authority of this intuitive emotionalism is beyond all questioning. At the crises of life reflection fails, and instinctive impulses control conduct, all the more determinative and imperious is this feeling because it is transitory. These commanding impulses are the highest peaks of life's experience. "And yet," the author says of Michael at the end, "though the disquieting delusion of life, sweet as it is, still clouds him, like a thin mist, now and then parting and unveiling immortal peaks, he goes his ways, joyful and confident, as one whom invisible Gods are leading." The mysterious emotional voices speak to men at the momentous turning points of life, and guide them aright. Michael's satisfaction is simply in his obedience to these inner guides; these are the invisible Gods.

Among the masterpieces of German romanticism is Arnim's unfinished novel "Die Kronenwächter" (The Guardians of the Crown), the story of an imperial idea maintained by a mysterious league down through the centuries. Possibly it was from this novel that Ricarda Huch, herself a thorough and illuminating student of the romantic epoch, took the cue for the story entitled "Von den Königen und der Krone" (Of the Kings and the Crown). In this novel she surrenders quite completely to the enchantment of romanticism; she has given us a story of modern days, veiled by a romantic mystery which suggests the magic of Novalis or Tieck.

On the shore of the Adriatic and in desolate mountain regions towering above it, there lives a race which still cherishes even in its present destitution the thought of its former grandeur, and still recognizes through the centuries the phantom sovereignty of an hereditary king. Humble labourers the men of this lordly race have become, and their king, Lastari, is one of the lowliest of them all. Yet back of the little cottage where he lives lies the cavern which keeps and hides the crown of generations of kings. The story is of Lastari and his children. In him, the royal blood is like a ferment, restlessly he wanders through life, ever seeking and never finding, unconscious of the source of his yearning.

As a young man he had married the daughter of a clan which had traditionally provided wives for the kings. On her death, recovering somewhat from the violence of his grief and his brooding melancholy, Lastari takes his three children and starts for the sea-coast. While her father sleeps, Surja, a queenly daughter of a race of kings, takes little Dragaino, and steals back to the place where their mother lies buried, to the place where the crown is kept. Lastari, with Lasko, a lad of seven years, continues the goalless journey which the four had begun together, and wanders out into the great world. He tries his hand at various employments; he even spends some years in Mexico where he marries a sensuous half-breed woman, the fatal error of his life. His talents, his natural gifts, his dignity and enterprise, lead him to temporary successes; fortunes are made but slip through his hands. He can not endure the monotonous application to routine; his interest flags when once the great scheme is launched. Consciously or unconsciously there wells up within him the craving of the persistent quest. Why should one continue to work in an oil factory when one is really a king? "It is certain that I have ruined my life," he says, looking back from middle-age, "although I have willed only the great and good, now it is impossible for me to reach the goal." "What goal?" queries Lasko, his son. Lastari does not know, yet even so he begs his son to seek it. After the crown is irretrievably lost, Lastari wants to go back to the mountains, to get the position of guard at the cave, to tell to visitors the story of the kings. Lasko, now rich and prominent, has difficulty in dissuading his father from this form of self-exhibition. Later still, a broken old man, Lastari leaves the shelter which Lasko has provided for him, and wanders as a minstrel through the mountain region, singing the songs of the vanished race of kings, his forefathers.

Soon after their return from America, **Lasko**, who had had some medical training there, obtains a position in a children's hospital at Lusinara. The founder of the hospital is an eccentric physician named Pius Reynegom. His brother Beatus is a manufacturer of great wealth. Lasko falls in love with Maielies, the daughter of the latter, and marries her. He turns now from a professional to a business life. Success and position are his, but the regal superstition, though quite unacknowledged, rules his sub-conscious being. There is always a conflict between his occupation and his real self. In Tieck's "Runenberg," the hero's soul has been subjected to a gradual process of crystallization through the one-time touch of a magic tablet on his hand; he cannot live the normal life of man, though he tries it for a time; there stirs within him that inner self which is his real destiny. So Lasko's life is only a kind of half-relationship to his environment. Even more half-natured is his marriage. Love, turbulent and passionate, moves Lasko at times, but often he can look at his wife almost through the eyes of a stranger. The tie which binds them year in, year out is the hope for the little boy "Divo," whom they dream of, talk about, but who never comes. Maielies becomes estranged, and listens to the love of her cousin Rizzo. After the indignant families have brought about the departure of the latter, Lasko and Maielies adopt an illegitimate son of Rizzo's; Maielies alone knows that Rizzo is the baby's father, neither knows who the mother was. But the mother, a

former servant in the household, is irresistibly
drawn toward the child and obtains the position
of his nurse. In dramatic scenes the truth is
disclosed. When Lasko is killed by his half-witted
brother, Zizito, the son of the Mexican half-
breed, Maielies clings to the adopted child, but
refuses to marry Rizzo. On a farm she cares
for the aged Lastari, who believes the little boy
to be his grandson, and thus the heir to the lost
crown.

For the crown itself had been lost long before
this, and the people of the mountain village
scattered. Rizzo had been the indirect cause.
Fascinated by the stories of the crown which
Lasko told, and spurred by the thirst for adventure, Rizzo goes to the mountains, ingratiates
himself with Surja and Dragaino by imperson-
ating Lasko, and together they plan a revolution
for the re-establishment of the kingdom. Their
secret is betrayed. Rizzo flees, Surja takes her
own life, and Dragaino, escaping to the coast
with the crown, is there surrounded by his foes.
He sails out on the sea, and then with the crown
in his hands he leaps into the water.

The story of the kings and their crown is a
modern version of the romantic fairy-tale. It
is written with a sovereign disregard for probabilities, and with sovereign inconsequence the
events follow one another. The popular fairy-
tale is naïvely logical; the supernatural is taken
for granted, but it is regulated by immutable laws
which are the product of primitive consciousness.
But the "Märchen" of the romanticists lacks all

such clearness of supernatural background. Its
characters are either acutely conscious of 'the
miraculous nature of their experience, or are quite
uncertain as to the difference between the natural
and the supernatural; they toy with the idea and
reflect upon it. For their philosophy gives them
no basis for reality. Even the fact of personal
identity is blurred to them. This latter incerti-
tude gives room for hints of palingenesis and
double personality. There is much of all this in
Ricarda Huch's novel. Lasko wavers in his distinctions between the real and the unreal. He
creates a figure out of his imagination simply to
deceive his father and then actually fears the
phantom of his own creating. He delights in
story-telling, and relates elaborate tales, giving
his remembrances out of former existences; these
may, of course, be repeated simply as an index
to Lasko's character, but there is more than a
suspicion that Lasko half-believes these fables,
that he is at times uncertain who he actually is.
Perhaps to minds pre-disposed to scientific interpretation, the whole tradition of the kingdom
and its influence may seem like a mere allegory
of the principle of heredity.

The story of Triumph Alley stands apart from
the other novels; it is different both in form and
content. The other three, despite their diversity,
due so largely to the opulence of picturesque detail, possess a distinct similarity of plot. The
action of "Ludolf Ursleu" and of "Vita Somnium Breve" is primarily concerned with a love
which is outside of wedlock; the obstacle to a

legitimate union of the lovers is removed, but the marriage does not take place; this same "fable" covers the most important single action in the decidedly episodical story of the kings and their crown. The incomprehensible, which is close to the supernatural, prevents the marriage of Ezard and Galeida. Michael Unger is led by invisible Gods to turn back after what seem to be the only obstacles to his union with Rosa have been overcome. In the last novel, no extrinsic causes are adduced to account for the obduracy of Maielies; perhaps it is her sense of duty to Lasko's father, perhaps the shock of Lasko's tragic death and a reminiscent fidelity which it occasioned, or the satisfaction of possessing a child of Rizzo's, even if it is not her own.

Such an identity in the essential elements of plot would seem to provide material for the establishment of a principle. Are we to infer that a passion of love, contravening traditional and established law, works in a circle and ultimately defeats itself? Or that its strength is less than that of other and legitimate affections, such as fatherhood? Or that substitutes may be found, perhaps a kind of vicarious child-bearing? Or that delay enjoined by a lingering regard for conventions, brings atrophy of passion? The novels themselves fail utterly to answer these questions. We cannot order the material so as to state from it an ethical formula. Life is an unsolved mystery. What we know of life is so infinitesimal compared with the infinitude of our ignorance that our profoundest questionings are childish play. Inscrutable impulses shape the destiny of man, impulses which come no-whence and go no-whither, like the wind which bloweth where it listeth. The higher development of man is in the direction of the irrational, at least, if by rational conduct we understand the result of conscious ratiocination; the farther a man removes himself from the duller average, the more completely is he governed by purely intuitive voices.

Thus Ricarda Huch chooses unusual characters, standing out from their fellows, because in this higher sense they are more representative of man in his advance from the brute. Characteristic of her fiction is the selection of an individual or a group of individuals who are distinctly abnormal. They belong to a peculiar and rarefied humanity. Just as birds through a different arrangement of the spectrum of the eye see things differently from men, as cats with a differing vision are often startled seemingly by a mysterious presence invisible to our unseeing eyes, so these gifted men and women are subjected to something outside normal human experience. The novelist places men and women of more than human beauty and more than human gifts in a confining and uncomprehending world, themselves never understanding their own superiority and incapable of a consistent use of it. More tragic then, because of this superiority, is the subjection of these sublimated heroes to the will of destiny. For upon an infinite checkerboard a nameless power moves its pieces, making apparently no difference between kings, and queens, and pawns, sacrificing them capriciously; no one has yet made out the rules of the game, and no one knows what its purpose is and what end it serves.

A resemblance to the typical heroes of early romanticism seems unmistakable; there men and women were presented who were possessed by some divine gift; they were poets like Heinrich von Ofterdingen, musicians and artists, intermediaries between the real world and the dream world, seers who revealed, or who seemed destined to reveal, the mysteries of time and eternity. Perhaps through a modern conception of human interests and values, Ricarda Huch assigns more practical occupations to her heroes; Michael, Ezard, and Lasko are all men of business affairs, though all three touch and pursue for a time other and more intellectual activities, medicine and biology; — the biologist may perhaps be regarded as the modern counterpart of the mediæval dreamer, as the modern seer. But they are all caught up by a splendid vision, are tormented into restlessness by the conviction that it ought to be possible to make life more glorious, incomparably more satisfying than it is. One of the early romanticists defined man as a finite thing developed into the infinite. With varying intensity, varying with life's vicissitudes, the consciousness of this relationship to infinity seizes the heroes of Ricarda Huch's novels, confuses them in a workaday world, and impels to an activity which neither they themselves nor any one else can really understand. And because the novelist herself has no definite conception of the goal of man's striving, she cannot lead her heroes to it. The pathos of blunted aspiration, like the transitoriness of beauty, lies heavily upon her, and casts shadows into her sunlight. In every case it is

"The high that proved too high, the heroic for
     earth too hard,
The passion that left the ground to lose itself
     in the sky."

But the conception of infinity works backwards as well as forwards; and this haunting sense of man's higher capabilities because of his participation in the infinite is linked to a consciousness of an infinite source, "the trailing clouds of glory." This is, it may be, the mystic symbolism of the kings and their crown. "What is the life of man?" cried Ludolf Ursleu, "Like drops of rain which fall from heaven upon the earth, we measure our span of time, driven this way and that by the wind of fate. Wind and fate have their immutable laws, in accordance with which they act but what does the drop know of them, the drop which they sweep on before them? With other drops it rushes through the air, till it can steal away in the sand. But heaven collects them all again unto itself and pours them down again and again, always the same drops, which nevertheless are different drops." Even this somewhat dispiriting hypothesis with which the world-weary monk answers his own question, allows for an activity in endlessness in connection with an endless power; it leaves room too for romantic conceptions of palingenesis and metempsychosis, and provides occult sources for the impulses of life.

The substance out of which these stories are
fashioned is indubitably of our place and day;
there is no vagueness in their geographical locali-
ties, and the whole fabric of human institutions
and relationships is that of our modern world.
But this persistent assumption that our conduct
at all determinative crises of life is guided by
utterly inexplicable forces imparts to them,
despite their contemporaneity, something of a
legendary quality. They haunt us like an obscure
mediæval allegory, or, perhaps more accurately,
like those baffling mediæval phantasies in which
the romanticists sought to embody their visions
of the unknown and the unknowable. One is reminded of an old allegorical painting to which the
clue has been lost,— the Urbino frescos of Piero
della Francesca, or some Florentine cassone front,
labeled "subject unknown;" the symmetry of
their design, the glory of their colouring, bewitch
us, we apprehend perhaps the general nature of
the incident portrayed, but we know that the
artist meant something more than what we
actually see. So we are possessed by a suspicion
that these tales contain a significance beyond the
mere surface record of the "fable." Even "Aus
der Triumphgasse," in ways which it is difficult
to analyze, shares this baffling characteristic; in
all the hideousness of its reality, we are perplexed
by the feeling that the same words which here
tell one story, might to him who knew the code,
convey another and a deeper meaning. But we
are afraid that even the author herself has lost
the code.

At a certain point in the development of Heinrich von Ofterdingen, the words of a friend open a secret door within him and he sees that his humble dwelling is built beside a sublime cathedral. Does our modern romanticist open such doors for us? Only in part, for there is a very modern absence of the steadying faith by which cathedrals were built. She is conscious of the greatness which surrounds us, but she is uncertain of its source, of its nature, and of man's relationship to it. To Ricarda Huch, man is surrounded by a translucent wall which no exertion of his energies has as yet made transparent. But she is a rebel against all purely materialistic conceptions of man's life; she refuses to admit the vanity of his striving. And if we ask what is the worth of it all, perhaps weary Farfalla comes the nearest to knowing the answer.

OMPTEDA AND THE ARISTOCRACY

A N aristocracy dependent on the maintenance of feudal privilege and prerogative faces competitive struggles in our modern world. During the nineteenth century, and conspicuously in the decades since the Franco-Prussian war, the life of the German nation had undergone a process of transformation through the creation of commercial and industrial values. Economic developments have undermined aristocratic prestige. The merchant prince rivals the prince of blood, or oftener outstrips him, in the display which traditionally divided the commoner from the noble; the commoner of egregious wealth elbows his way into the foreground and challenges the nobleman to stand beside him,— and quite naturally, since he himself has created the prevailing system of interests and values.

Then further, an aristocracy which derives its position from seignioral domains must, in the course of the centuries, encounter a perplexity of its own and nature's creating. The dependents on the harvests from ancestral acres increase in number by a defective but nevertheless appalling geometrical progression, and the estates become incapable of supporting the multiplied progeny. The provision of respectable employment for the offspring of the nobility, sufficient to sustain life and dignity, has been a service of the military establishment; this acutely realized necessity has its direct economic relationship to the existence

131

of a large armed force requiring a multitude of officers. And the army system is maintained and furthered by a government largely controlled by those who have this insidious interest in its continuance and enlargement.

Georg, Freiherr von Ompteda is the scion of a noble house, once prominent at the Hanoverian court, and is a retired officer of the Prussian army; thus he interprets these interrelated and largely identical aristocracies of blood and arms. Some of his stories, indeed, deal not at all or only insignificantly with these chosen segments of German social life, and, in view of his bewildering fecundity, it would be strange if this were not the case. "Excelsior," for example, is a tale of Alpine climbing; "Philister über dir" (The Philistines are upon Thee) the story of an artist wedded to a woman of uncomprehending mediocrity and frivolity, and his "Monte Carlo" is a pallid companion to Dostoievsky's "Gambler." These, and others are perhaps not entirely negligible evidences of versatility, but Ompteda's chief merit consists in the frankness and sympathy with which he portrays a social class which, despite the alleged revelations of popular story-tellers, has lived its life behind closed doors. Ompteda's observations of the class into which he was born and in whose circles he has spent his years form the chief substance of his novels; now and then he makes deductions from his accumulated observations and seasons his material with the salt of his convictions. To a group of three novels,

"Sylvester von Geyer," "Eysen," and "Cäcilie
von Sarryn," the novelist gave the collective title
"Deutscher Adel um 1900;" the title itself suggests his definite purpose, and the three stories
constitute Ompteda's most determined effort to
grasp and hold in its entirety the complicated
problem of the aristocracy at the turning point
of the centuries.

Of the three, "Eysen" is the most important,
a really notable novel. "Eysen" is the name of
one of those East-Elbian families whose life is
so inextricably entwined with the growth of Prussia. Founded on a knightly battle-field, it has
provided countless officers for the Prussian army,
and, in times of peace, its statesmen have stood
with steadying hand at the ship's helm. The
tradition of service to the state holds the Eysens
with unyielding grip. Indirectly through the
fruits of their service they have become in a
certain sense stock-holders in the great Prussian
enterprise, and believe that their representative
power in Prussian affairs should be commensurate
with their accumulated investments. It is
Ompteda's purpose to relate the story of this
family through a period of fifteen years at the
end of the century.

The two volumes of the novel are each supplied with an appendix consisting of pages clipped
from the Almanach de Gotha, actually imitating
the print and paging of that august annual. A
comparison of the two appendices reveals much
of the substance of the "plot;" obviously much
of what happens to the characters is indicated

there, but the device is, at the outset, a distinct aid to the reader who uses this kind of character-index after the fashion of a play-bill. The novelist too, fortified by the concrete information thus baldly stated, may relieve the introductory pages of some explanatory material, which, in view of the extensive ramifications of the Eysen family, might make the early chapters seem like a selection from the Book of Deuteronomy. The story is without hero or heroine except for the collective and composite entity called the family. To appraise adequately the novelist's success in managing a really multitudinous company and in interweaving a half dozen different narratives into a unit, some indication of the attempted scope of the story will be worth while.

At the opening of the story the acknowledged head of the family is Heinrich von Eysen, a retired minister of state, a man of commanding personality and of distinguished service. He is a childless widower. Ompteda makes him the mouth-piece of much of his own thought. Next to him stands his nephew Ernst, a country squire with three children, Gisela, a daughter, and two sons who as cadets are preparing for service in the army. Another nephew, Fabian, serves as "Hofchef" to the Prince of Sarnheim-Resa, and likewise has two sons and a daughter. A third nephew is a distinguished professor at the university, and has three sons. Another still is Rudolf, a Major in the Prussian service, with one son; Ludwig, another nephew, has already stepped aside from traditional pathways, and is

a merchant in Hamburg; his wife was a Cuban
beauty, and they have three children. The list
of nephews closes with Cäsar, who, to the horror
of the family, has become an actor. There are
in addition three nieces, one of them married to
Graf Eysen, the chief representative of another
branch of the family.

That Ompteda moves this multitude through
a period of fifteen years, and disposes ap-
propriately of these and more than these, is a
triumph of considerable dimensions. An external
device whereby the characters are first introduced,
and then at convenient seasons are "rounded up,"
as it were, and accounted for, is the family dinner, held every five years at a hotel in Berlin.
The story begins with one of these; the novelist,
favouring the weakness of our memories, provides
a diagram of the seating at the table. A second
dinner is described near the centre of the story,
and a third dinner closes the book, affording an
opportunity for retrospection and conclusion both
for the characters themselves and for the reader.
Though a formula of this sort leads the novelist
into repetitions, the device serves its purpose
neatly.

"Sylvester von Geyer" is much less ambitious
in its plan, but because of the engaging portrait
of the hero, it is more appealing as a story.
Ompteda has chosen here the fortunes of the
"army nobility" as his theme. In the course of
time, the numbers increasing with each generation, these "army families" have sundered all
ties with the ancestral lands from which they

sprang; a theoretical connection is perhaps maintained, which brings whatever satisfaction may be derived from so impalpable a privilege. They share only the family heritage of responsibility without any of its material blandishments; poverty, relative poverty at any rate, sits at their boards. Their participation, however, in the profession of arms has become so fixed as to create a caste of almost unbending rigidity. Instinctively the sons follow their fathers' footsteps and the daughters see only an officer's uniform down the uncertain pathway of hope.

The story of Sylvester is a very simple one. Like many a novel which the world has learned to count among its masterpieces, it begins with the birth of its hero, with the wistful, solemnly gay company which surrounds his cradle. Sylvester is the son of a retired captain; he opens his eyes upon a world of love and care, of discipline and deprivation; he goes to school and has picturesque encounters with incarnate pedagogy; he is obstinate, willful, and naughty, but altogether lovable. Later Sylvester enters the military academy,—the Geyers seek the army as the rivers seek the sea,— and the chapters of his life as a cadet may rank in freshness and appeal among the best records of school-boy days. He enters the army as an ensign, and the scene shifts to barracks and drill field; he falls in love foolishly, and for a time he trails about on the edges of a society which is not his and never can be; he learns to conquer self, to work, to seek for abiding values in a complex and shifting world,

and — dies; Sylvester's untimely death we can
hardly forgive his creator, even on the plea that
it saved him from a marriage of true love, which
would, however, have reproduced the pinched
circumstances and straitened opportunities of
his father's house.

"Cäcilie von Sarryn" is the least significant of
the series; it bears a less certain message, and
its relationship to the general plan is somewhat
slender. The novel is a wholesome, homely story
on the trite theme of the reward in self-sacrifice.
The heroine, it is inferred, is the least attractive
of the four daughters of General von Sarryn,
since, at the opening of the story, she alone has
passed the normal time for marriage in her circles
without securing a husband,—and she becomes in
the course of time, a humdrum, decidedly un-
romantic old maid. The married sisters in their
several homes provide material for effective contrasts, and at the same time, their diverse needs
afford ripening and ennobling experiences for
Cäcilie herself. She is a kind of family stop-gap,
who fits without murmuring into the dull and
wearisome spaces of domestic calamities. It is
she who cares for the ageing general; and later,
when one sister and her husband are killed in a
railway accident, the family council assigns to
Cäcilie the burdensome task of "mothering" the
six children whom they leave behind. With
Cäcilie's positive heroism in accepting this burden, a great renunciation is linked, for Ompteda
makes the tragic accident coincident with Cäcilie's
one real love affair; it is a spinster's love for a

widower with several children, but to her it was her one promise of happiness.

The whole story of "Eysen" centres in the familiar notion of *noblesse oblige*. The aged minister of state emphasizes this principle by example and admonition; at the first family dinner he urges upon the young Eysens the obligation of earning their inheritance, their patent of nobility, ever anew, an idea which in one form or another is constantly on his lips. And when he is gone, the leadership of the family and the words of exhortation are passed on to Rudolf, Major von Eysen. The death of the great statesman is, by the way, clumsily contrived to fall on the same day with that of his master, the old Emperor, a piece of fictional clap-trap, quite unworthy of the novel; Herzog, another novelist who ought to know better, makes,— in "Der Graf von Gleichen,"—a similarly extraneous and specious use of the death of Bismarck. Major von Eysen, capable, conscientious, and efficient, is advanced to a generalship on his own substantial merits, thus fulfilling the behests of his uncle's creed which he has made his own. His cousin Emil, the professor, is one of the world's great physicians, honoured on four continents; in selfless recognition of the great principle, he uses his almost princely professional income in unacknowledged philanthropies. On Ludwig, the merchant, the family look somewhat askance, as upon an apostate; it does not appear quite certain whether or not the statesman is ready to include mercantile activities in the gospel of work which he enjoins

upon the younger Eysens, but, when years have
sobered and chastened the Eysen clan, Major
von Eysen, as his successor, expressly commends
such effort. Cäsar has used his native abilities
in a way alien to the family experience; in the
first excerpt from the Almanach de Gotha, there
is no mention of Cäsar's profession, though his
existence as an individual is duly recorded; and
the statesman is filled with consternation at the
mere thought of his appearing on the stage in
Berlin. But, nevertheless, Cäsar has evidently
dealt with the talent given him quite in the
spirit of the old man's principle, and his merits
are recognized through the grant of a "Hofrat"
title. This is an ornament to the second clipping
from the Almanach de Gotha, though with traditional discretion the stately annual does not record the nature of the service which merited this
distinction.

It must be noted, however, that the principle
of *noblesse oblige* suffers in some cases curious
distortions and limitations; it is obviously possible
for one to decline complete responsibility and to
retain only such traditional aspects of the obligation as suit one's convenience or pleasure. Count
and Countess von Eysen, for example, recognize
only the obligation to present a glittering show
to the outer world; their life is a medley of balls,
dinners, and races, governed by the effort to
cultivate exalted acquaintances and to scrutinize
the less exalted so as to avoid them. But the
exhibitional aspect of aristocratic obligation has
become relatively insignificant both in view of

the ingratitude of the bourgeois or proletarian spectator, and because of the distinguished success with which the wealthy commoner parades his magnificence. Fabian, the "Hofchef," consumes his life as a kind of sublimated butler to a petty ruling prince, in greasing the wheels of an utterly purposeless household. The Prince, and Princess of Sarnheim-Resa are amiable nonentities, loitering on the pathway to their pompous mausoleum; there is no assignable reason, not even a governmental one, for the existence of the prince or his court, and Fabian is a pathetically useless appendage to all this concentrated uselessness.

The natural numerical increase of an aristocratic family, the mathematical "sum total," is diminished, in the course of the years, not only by death but by defections. This latter partial disintegration of the aristocracy is brought about by two classes of renegades, those who wantonly disregard the principle of *noblesse oblige* and go to ruin, and those who purposely and consciously resign from the *noblesse* and hence deny the peculiar nature of its obligations, while embracing perhaps a general human principle of a similar kind. Ompteda illustrates these processes.

The familiar words, for example, are quite meaningless to Lieutenant Christl, the eldest son of Squire Ernst. His conduct brings disgrace upon himself, and distress and actual deprivation upon his family. From the smart races of his cavalry regiment Christl descends by easy stages to the unlovely company of commercial jockeydom, chooses worthless companions of both sexes, shuns the path of rectitude; and his honoured name becomes a newspaper byword. He finds a refuge in far-away Chicago where he marries a woman of forty-four with a suspicion of negro blood,— thus becoming a blot on the family annals and a disquieting memory. The weight of his delinquency rests heavily upon the family; his father pays the accumulation of unworthy debts, and dies broken-hearted. Financial difficulties force the sale of the ancient family seat; the widow and her daughter seek inexpensive quarters in Berlin, and Fabian, the second son, giving up his career in the army, actually accepts employment as a salaried overseer on the estate of his fathers, now in other hands.

Forgetfulness of the principle eliminates also Amélie, the daughter of the "Hofchef" to the Prince of Sarnheim-Resa. She elopes with a worthless adventurer, albeit one with a military title, and thus vanishes from the family chronicle, and incidentally from the Almanach de Gotha.

Voluntary resignation from the aristocracy is represented by Fedor, the eldest son of Professor von Eysen. He causes the family much pain and chagrin, but in a very different way from the antics of the gay lieutenant, and his end in suicide is perhaps, from the family point of view, more tragic than Christl's retirement to Chicago. One perceives at the opening dinner that some evil is to befall Fedor, for, until admonished by Lieutenant Christl, then a mere cadet, he fails to rise when the toast to the King of Prussia is proposed.

Fedor is stirred, even as a school-boy, to indignant
sympathy with the lower classes, which involves
a complete repudiation of the class to which he
himself belongs. At eighteen, he has written a
brochure entitled "The Nobles and the Fourth
Estate," filled apparently with half-baked ideas
and revolutionary sentiments, yet effectively rein-
forced by accurate observations among his own
kinsfolk.

As head of the family, the aged statesman takes
Fedor to task for his unseasoned vapourings.
The interview occupies nearly twenty pages, and
in itself proves that Ompteda is not merely writing a story. Baron von Eysen's admonitions are
in part merely a repetition of his address at the
family dinner; there he had reminded the young
Eysens of their origins, and showed that, generation after generation, the Eysens had earned a
right to their noble name, had with blood and
iron confirmed their nobility; he urged the continuance of this obligatory endeavour, even if in
modest measure, yet commensurate with one's
gifts. Fedor, when once aroused and, as it were,
liberated, vents the ferment of his soul in a torrent of invective, and scornfully excoriates the
whole aristocratic system. "Why" he asks again
and again, "should I be privileged to exalt myself
above the multitude because a thousand years ago
one of my ancestors was a man of parts? Why
should an idiot because a count by birth be more
than an artisan's son, who can perform imperishable services for mankind?" With restrained
emotion the old man listens to Fedor's seething

tirade, and then begins to explain and refute.
To the social ruin which his nephew proposes,
which, according to the boyish iconoclast, is already upon us, the minister opposes the solidity
of the existing order; and the heritage of other
days is only the more glorious because it imposes
the necessity of continual constructive labour,
because it has the inherent capability of adapting
itself to a fluid civilization.

To Fedor's fundamental criticism that the
nobility forms a separate class, in and for itself, simply by right of birth, with privileges
and material distinctions due solely to that
right, the statesman makes a characteristic
and curious reply: "Let each nobleman win for
himself his nobility, that is, in an ideal sense.
In the last analysis it is in this world not a matter of seeming but of being. Many a man is at
large who has shown that he has the mind of
a scoundrel; is he less a scoundrel because there
is no law which punishes the possessor of such
a mind? However unworthy a count may be
of the title he bears, it cannot be taken from
him, unless he has committed some legal offense,
but is that a reason why he should be picked
out for special reprobation because he still bears
the title?" Fedor seems to feel the raggedness
of this reasoning, which obviously fails entirely
to meet his objection,— though one would hesitate to suggest that his uncle is disingenuous or
purposely deceptive,—but Fedor has neither the
poise of mind nor the emotional control to make
adequate reply. Like many a man when in-

tellectually at bay, he turns to the *argumentum
ad hominem,* and slashes away at vulnerable
points in the Eysen clan.

When Professor von Eysen dies, Fedor scan-
dalizes the family by interrupting the services
at the grave; he delivers a brief address on his
father's character and achievements, naturally
not failing to introduce some hints of his own
conception of values; this incident is especially
mortifying because of the distinguished company
present, which includes the Prussian crown-prince.
Now Fedor spurns financial help, and declares
his will to struggle with the mass of mankind
for his daily bread, sharing the common lot.
The story of Fedor's efforts to earn a living,
of his disillusionment, of the bitterness and scepticism which take the place of his dreams of a
redeemed world, is a brief one. Fedor takes
poison. The utter futility of his own repudia-
tions, he comes himself to realize; even as a
vagabond, the inherited instincts of his class cling
to him; he cannot join the class to which he was
not born, nor return to the one which he has
forsaken. Ompteda has constructed the story
of Fedor to prove that the salvation of the
aristocracy does not consist in a wholesale repudiation of privilege and obligation; the perplexities of a serious-minded, conscience-troubled
noble are not eliminated by erasions in the Almanach de Gotha.

Uncle Gottfried in "Sylvester von Geyer" is
another example of unsuccessful apostasy. He
obstinately defied the family tradition and re-

fused to become a soldier. Caught up by the flood of democratic thinking in the mid-century, he actually fought among the deluded children of freedom at the barricades of '48. This delinquency constitutes a formidable family skeleton, and Sylvester himself never hears of it till in his young manhood when he is securely buttoned up in "his majesty's uniform." Latent artistic talents were stifled by family prejudice, and Gottfried, in refusing to become a soldier, incidentally did not become anything else. He shuffles along in shabby bachelordom, a kindly, humorous critic of life, who acknowledges the existence of a mistake somewhere, either in himself or society, though he has long ago given up any effort to find it. He only reasons out for himself a kind of fatalism: "after all, we can not get rid of the blood that runs in our veins, or the atmosphere in which we were reared."

On the other hand, Sylvester's father might seem to contribute a very concrete and indisputable refutation of the tradition which thrusts the sons of officers indiscriminately into their fathers' military boots. For some of them, despite heredity and environment, display various and sundry degrees of unfitness for the service. Poor Captain von Geyer has given his fatherland years of faithful service; but apparently from the professional point of view, he has never really satisfied any one but himself, and that not always. Hence his retirement to irritated, disgruntled idleness on an insufficient pension resulted from a double dissatisfaction. He

can hardly be called a supernumerary, certainly
not a "mute" in the family drama, which grows
more tense after his retirement because of increased financial limitations; he fidgets in de-
sultory fashion about writing a history of the
family, or of his old regiment, but he has neither
the energy nor the talent for the work, his only
real equipment being a pride of participation.
Is there then no hope for the military aristocracy
either in acquiescence or rebellion?

The third novel also contains an apostate from
the aristocratic faith, two of them indeed. One
of the two Ranghofen lads, Cäcilie's wards, falls
into evil ways, forgets his rank in lowly and degrading companionships, and is saved indeed
from the last step of folly only by the picturesque
interference of his doughty old-maid aunt. The
other apostate is the humorous figure of Anastasia, née Princess of Roiningen-Althaus, who jests
brutally and bluntly about the class which she has
forsaken in order to wed a Rhenish manufacturer
with countless millions. She expressly provides in
her will that none of the money shall ever fall
into the hands of a reigning prince of Roiningen-
Althaus, a provision calculated to vex her recal-
citrant nephew, the reigning prince, while favouring his brother, who becomes the husband of Lily
von Ranghofen. Since the "reigning" of this
mediatised prince is somewhat microscopic in
quantity, and her money nevertheless serves to
bolster up impoverished members of the aristocracy,— Lily and her husband,— the defection of
Anastasia becomes merely whimsical and mean-

ingless; it is only a beneficent arrangement whereby Aunt Anastasia is sent out into the capitalistic
world to acquire a fortune for two amiable characters in the novel.

There is, on the other hand, considerable compensation for losses in an aristocracy; both the
numbers and the diminishing material fortunes
of the aristocracy are strengthened by occasional
accretions from the capitalistic class. Such a
fortunate recruiting from the bourgeoisie is perhaps symbolized by the grant of a baronial title
to young Gideon, who marries Gisela von Eysen.
The marriage is incidentally a pleasant tit bit for
the sentimental reader, since it restores the Ernst
Eysen family to their lost domain, for Gideon is
the purchaser of the estate. His father had been
a modern captain of industry, but Gideon himself
feels attracted to the profession of country gentleman; luckily his paternal inheritance is sufficient to allow the cultivation of his preferences.
To meet the requirements more satisfactorily, he
acquires the title of baron through a mercantile
transaction the exact nature of which is not disclosed. Gideon spends a year in travel, mainly
to allow the "grass to grow over" his sudden rise
in rank; then, sending up his new baronial visiting card, he becomes the somewhat obviously successful suitor for Gisela's hand.

The wedding party is Ompteda's most noteworthy confrontation of the two aristocracies, the
old aristocracy of blood and the new aristocracy
of gold, who for the most part glare at one another over hedges of convention,— the lion now

become largely decorative and ineffective, and the beast of burden with its inappropriate trappings. Ompteda allows the didactic, or at any rate, the expository to run afoul of his epic, and records in full the after-dinner speeches of Gideon's brother, a *Kommerzienrat* by the way, and of Rudolf, now General von Eysen. To the astonishment of the Eysens, the *Kommerzienrat* asserts that the new alliance is not a matter of pride to his family; and his method of developing his position is even more disconcerting. He recounts the services of the nobility in building up the greatness of the common fatherland, but so objective an appraisement of their virtues from a commoner, a merchant and manufacturer, offends the Eysens; it implies the right to evaluate and criticise; they anticipate also the inevitable "but," which is not long in coming; other classes, namely, have contributed and are contributing to the common weal. A new kind of pride of class, even a pride of the firm, shimmers through the words of the speaker. It makes the Eysens uneasy. He says openly that his brother's baronial title is to him neither an elevation nor a betterment, every workman in his employ is a "man" alike worthy with his own son; the only real test of life is in striving to be something and to do something. The speech of General von Eysen is cut from the same block as the utterances of his dead uncle. He insists that the only justification for pride is in progress, and, if one is already favoured by circumstance, in yielding all the more fruit; that the work of the living is the necessary supplement and complement to the labour of other generations; and the obligation to work, whatever the task may be, makes all men equal. To the assembled Eysens he even commends the Gideon family as a pattern of efficiency. The frankness of the commoner appeared embarrassingly tactless to the Eysen clan, but luckily their representative was exceedingly diplomatic, and the tension was released. Those who could not accept the substance of the General's speech as really establishing any basis of equality, or find a temporary excuse for it in the present social event, could see in it an almost regal type of courtesy, which both gives and takes, and to the seeing eye takes more than it gives, hence they let it pass as a graceful condescension, and began to be agreeable to their guests.

Thus new blood filters into the aristocracy, but often it brings no appreciable increment of material possessions, leaving its value less easy of appraisement. The record of gain and loss goes on. A closer reading of the pages from the Almanach de Gotha betrays several family condescensions, attritions, if not delinquencies, even before the opening of the story. Amid the chaos of counts, barons, Knights of St. John, ladies-in-waiting, and the like, several names are hidden away which lack even the sacred "von," and one blatantly bourgeois Müller has been smuggled in.

If the aristocracy maintains the military system with one eye on the defence of the fatherland and the other, unconsciously perhaps, on a satisfactory employment for its sons, at any rate it does not choose a sinecure for them. This cycle of

novels, supported by many others, presents very
concretely Ompteda's conception of the German
army officer. Sylvester von Geyer and his friend
Eldenfleth often talk of their life and prospects
in a way which suits well the novelist's purpose
of exposition. They can not fashion their lives
as they will; they are incomparably more ham-
pered than most men in the control of life's details. An impecunious clerk can enjoy himself
in his own lowly way, can distribute his income
according to the emphasis of his tastes, he can
ask whom he will to share his beggarly lot. But
the young officer is bound to the wheel of an inflexible system; it demands his obedience in all
things, even in the affairs of the heart; it commands hard work with remorseless and unfailing
detection of incapacity or negligence; it requires
of him a personal presentability which eats up
his stipend and invites debt;— when one of those
familiar momentary silences falls upon a company, the Germans are wont to say: "An angel
sweeps through the room," or "A lieutenant has
paid his debts," attributing perhaps a flavour of
the unusual or even the miraculous to either event.
The system is argus-eyed and peers inquisitively
into every concern of life; it stands remorselessly
listening at every key-hole.

According to Ompteda the typical German officer rises splendidly to the ideal requirements of
his function. He is keenly alive to the cultural
and moral responsibilities which he assumes toward the collective youth of the country; he is to
train sturdy, honest, efficient, and clean-minded

men; and in the solemnity of this obligation he
acts as a father to simple and sometimes wayward children. Beneath the most frowning ex-
terior, the ram-rod bearing, lies a heart of tender
consideration. Sylvester stands in boyish awe of
his superiors, who distribute their criticisms inex-
orably and at times with blunt vigour, but the
novelist rarely fails to disclose their tenderness,
their solicitude, their real affection for their military fledglings. The hero of Ompteda's later
novel, "Herzeloïde" is perhaps the most perfect
and the most purposeful portrait of such a fatherly officer, but there are many companions both in
the cycle and out of it, as in "Normalmenschen,"
where an older officer turns the subaltern from a
pathway of folly.

Ompteda would enter a word also for the democracy under the unavoidably mechanical and
impersonal discipline. A democracy of comradeship may follow from a democracy of service. In
"Sylvester von Geyer" a lieutenant from a smart
cavalry regiment is placed in the same room at
the "Kriegsschule" with three infantry-men, two
of whom, Sylvester and his friend Eldenfleth, are
as poor as church mice; real friendship develops
from this enforced intimacy, and later the smart
lieutenant joins these two impecunious comrades
in a trip on the Rhine, succumbing to their niggardly method of travelling and quailing not at
their shabby civilian clothes. The lists of Sylvester's comrades at the cadet school are by no
means composed entirely of members of the aristocracy; many officers at his garrison are frankly

of middle class origins, but in both cases Ompteda is zealous in asserting, there is no standard applied except that of efficient work.

Worldliness and vice, arrogance and brutality, are not entirely painted out in Ompteda's picture, but they are reduced to innocuous dimensions,— are perhaps like natural defects in the pigment which interest the connoisseur and do not constitute a real blemish. The "king's coat" is but a symbol for a higher responsibility; and, since the officer, by his wearing of it, stands out from the mass, is a "city set on a hill," so must his conduct be worthy of his eminence, and the shadow of reproach must not darken his uniform or that for which it stands. The "other side" of German army life is better known in this country through novel and play; evil tidings travel faster, it is said, than good; slander or merited rebuke and censure take to themselves wings which fear no ocean's breadth. There have been sensational successes in German fiction, which, perhaps because of official disapproval or prohibition, have assumed the importance of revelations; such was Lieutenant Bilse's "Aus einer kleinen Garnison" (From a Small Garrison) which, with its less familiar companion "Lieb' Vaterland," presented the army garrisons as veritable sinks of iniquity, the officers as callous brutes, efficient leaders in every evil. Beyerlein's "Jena oder Sedan?" was built on larger lines and was instinct with sincerity; the author's purpose was one of denunciation and of warning; does not the German army, glutted with the pride of past achievement, a glittering, soulless machine, face a disaster like Jena rather than a victory like Sedan? And to Beyerlein, the officers are largely responsible for the military degeneracy; he charges them with shameless presumption and insolence, with crass brutality, with petty and gross vices; their very existence as a powerful and privileged class is a menace.

By championing a democracy of labour, in which the scions of noble houses are to participate, regardless of the nature of work and mindful only of its quality, Ompteda makes a signal concession to prevailing ideas of economic values and human obligation; he takes a significant step forward toward a solution for the problem of his class. On the other hand the novelist has nothing to say, at any rate nothing important to say, about the daughters of aristocratic families in their relationship to altered economic and social systems. He is silent, inconclusive, or by implication, reactionary. Since the weaker sex predominates in "Cäcilie von Sarryn," one might expect to find there the novelist's deliberate effort to cope with the woman question as far as it concerns the women of his social stratum; one might hope to find a sincere and honest statement of the problem, as for example in Gabriele Reuter's "Aus guter Familie." But in the case of Cäcilie herself, and her four nieces, or of Sylvester's three sisters, Ompteda hardly does more than provide material for discussion, and somewhat meagre material at that; he merely scratches the surface of the question, and with a complacence which borders on the naïve. For the daughters of gentle birth he suggests no activity outside the home; marriage is the *summum bonum* for them all, and for the unfortunates left waiting on the marriage-mart when the little day of barter and bidding is over, there will be, it is hoped, some quiet pathways of usefulness provided, even if the provision be not due to such a beneficent accident as that which made Cäcilie von Sarryn the foster-mother to six children. The family responsibility in the case of the daughters has not advanced beyond the aboriginal effort to secure husbands for them.

One must infer, however, that Ompteda feels a positive distaste for the formal organization of society which provides a kind of auction market for marriageable daughters,— parents arranging a series of exhibitions under the guise of social diversion. No one of the seven or eight heroines involved obtains a husband in this way. Ida von Ranghofen marries a second cousin from the Rhine country who accidentally appears on the scene for a visit. Lily's husband, the brother of the mediatised prince, is a regimental comrade of the aforesaid second cousin, and falls in love with Lily at her sister's wedding. Two of Sylvester's sisters are provided for through Sylvester's regimental friends; he brings one home for a brief visit, and the first wedding breeds the second. Love at first sight, primarily at other people's weddings, appears in almost childlike simplicity as Ompteda's primitive solution of the difficulty. The eldest of the Ranghofens, by the way, fails to acquire a husband in either way; she grows angular in mind and rotund in body, till a temporary absence of her aunt opens up for her the solace of household duties. From the last dinner of the Eysens, that solemn meeting of young and old where the problems of life and death for the noble family are to be discussed, Ompteda expressly excludes the women altogether. They have no place in the family counsels; they are still unripe for anything except a domestic participation in family misfortunes. Martha is still the patron saint of German womanhood. In other words, the daughters of the aristocracy have as yet found no accepted method of leaving the protecting and stultifying shelter of traditions. They are supposed to fold their hands, when misfortune overtakes them, and submit to restrictions in opportunity, although a little effort of their own might open up to them incomparable enlargements of life.

It is easy to scorn or ridicule an hereditary aristocracy; its very existence may seem an irritating anachronism. It is harder, but, in the modern world, perhaps equally fitting to pity the children of feudal privilege. The restless waves of a new social order are gradually engulfing the house in which they dwell. The novelist tries to bring us into a keener appreciation of their perplexities; by disclosures which show a reconciling system of compensations, he would silence the voice of uncomprehending censure. Even if members of the aristocracy are indifferent to the criticism of those who are socially beneath them, they cannot be entirely callous either to the relative diminishing of their material resources or indeed to the insistent clamour of those who would distribute their still considerable possessions. The very decrease of their wealth as a class compels them to cling more tenaciously to their imponderables, which, indeed, were they so minded, they would find difficult either to destroy or to give away. Hence as long as they find them useful, they are busy inventing excuses for retaining them. Their record of distinguished service to the fatherland is offered as an answer to revolutionary mutterings. And for the most part, it would seem, the German aristocracy has not forgotten its traditional obligations. One sometimes gathers the impression from an English novel that the British aristocracy has advanced to a kind of sophisticated idleness; it becomes, to be sure, democratic at times but of sheer *ennui*, and invites the upper and more opulent levels of the *bourgeoisie* to play upon its shaded castle lawns, thus introducing a kind of golden age, which apparently is not one of innocence. Ompteda is eager that no such impression shall prevail concerning the German aristocracy; and for a plausible documentation of this defence he surely deserves the gratitude of his kind.

Ompteda is distinctly a realist in his methods of work; he belongs, one may perhaps say, to the school of Fontane. His theme is modern society, and when once the exclusiveness of his social class is granted, he takes his material from the commonplace and everyday in character and circumstance. Indeed, his work lacks those half romantic characteristics which to some critics,— accord‚ ing to their conception of realism,— might seem to invalidate Fontane's leadership. His novels have no lyric undertones, sounding faintly and perhaps fitfully through the story and haunting the memory when the book is closed; he makes no use of romantic premonitions nor of sympathetic backgrounds in nature. He is also decidedly more impersonal than Fontane in his attitude toward the story which he is telling. Though his sympathy with his own social class is plain, though he likes his characters, is interested in them, and is himself entertained by what he tells of them, one can hardly say that he has created a single character,— with the exception of Sylvester von Geyer, which is probably in part autobiographical, — whose destiny deeply stirs him, and he has difficulty, as a consequence, in communicating to his readers anything like vital concern or partisanship.

Though the elements of Ompteda's plots seem to contain potentialities for gripping conflicts, through contrariety of desire and purpose, the novelist rarely allows a situation to develop into emotional intensity. There are no really thrilling scenes. No one is possessed by an overmastering passion; giant will does not clash with giant will. There are no villains, and only now and then is any one really culpably naughty. The great and moving passions, love and ambition, envy, hatred, malice, and all uncharitableness, are smoothed out to a duller level. In Fontane's "Ellernklipp" father and son love the same girl;

jealousy masters the father, and he throws his son and rival from the cliff to certain destruction on the rocks below, a scene of compelling verity and tragic power; envy leads Fabian, the "Hofchef" to the Prince of Sarnheim-Resa, to quarrel with another official, and he falls in a duel which results from the disagreement; but the event is so circumscribed by petty formalities, so smothered in the incredible pettiness of the microscopic court, that the tragedy loses most of its poignancy. There is a touch of real pathos when Christl, the renegade lieutenant, and his heart-sick father eat their last meal together in Hamburg before Christl's embarking for America; it represents, however, a relatively low point in the emotional scale; one needs only to compare it with such simple but overwhelming scenes as that, for example, in Fontane's "L'Adultera," where Melanie is scorned by her own daughter, or in "Effi Briest," where Effi sees the child from whom her own sin has severed her. One feels the tragic pulse-beat of the world when in "Irrungen, Wirrungen" Lene parts from her lover: "And I shall never hold your hand in mine!" Cäcilie von Sarryn looks quizzically at the professor's picture, which she had bought, and puts it in the fire; it represented a dream of domestic activity, of a focus for expenditure of energy, which was shattered; it was not the collapse of an irreplaceable life-element.

To what extent this absence of intensity in the issues of life, this relative inertness and quiescence, contributing a certain sluggishness to the movement of his plots, is due to the traditional

reticences and inhibitions which hold the class of
Ompteda's choosing, seems largely indeterminate;
the counter-evidence of history, of drama and
story, would have to be weighed before a trustworthy verdict were possible. The caste system
does indeed confine men within traditional spheres
of activity, in a certain sense thus simplifying the
problems of life. But one might expect an increased intensity due to concentration; the more
nearly impossible an escape from the barriers of
caste, the more vigorous one might suppose that
the struggle would be inside the enclosure. And
yet, unquestionably, a certain monotonous pla-
cidity marks the career of most noblemen. To
so many of them a large part of life is completely
fore-ordained, so mapped and charted from the
outset, that individual initiative suffers partial or
complete atrophy. From the awakening of babyhood on, the predestination becomes a part of developing consciousness, ineradicable and unquestioned. As the system offers safeguards against
disintegration, so it presents only a modicum of
incentive. The typical aristocrat is not likely to
be at war with himself, for the system tends to
smother any rebellious individualism long before
it gains control; theoretically at least, and to an
extent practically, he has little cause for controversy with members of his own class, for each has
his own niche or groove which he accepts as a
kind of cosmic arrangement quite beyond question.
Nor does he, except when forced, enter into conflict with organized society, the constitution of
which is so largely to his advantage. Intense con-

servatism, particularly when solidly entrenched in material safeguards, is largely a negative and inactive principle.

Here too, the military establishment, moulding generation after generation with insistence and re-iteration, contributes its influence. In spite of the testimony of sensational novels, presenting examples of individual insubordination and emotional ferment, the discipline of the barracks suppresses initiative and individuality both in officers and men; it enjoins conformity and uniformity; the issues of life are predetermined, many of them with a finality which one does not presume to question. The very capacity for questioning is taken away. Indubitably also the general dulness of the material, the tranquillity of movement in Ompteda's stories, are in part ascribable to the relatively low conception of woman's place in his world of ambition and conflict. In the midst of a literature steeped in sex hysterics, it is at least a relief to find stories built up out of other interests. Yet it is a disappointment that the novelist deals so complacently, for the most part merely nominally, with woman's share in the tumult of life. Ompteda's women are neither gifted with quickening ideas nor mastered by passions; nor are they the centres of passionate conflict; no "topless towers" are ever burned because of them. Ompteda has lost the romantic attitude toward woman's influence in the affairs of life, and has not yet gained the sociological.

Life is a much more complex matter than one would infer from Ompteda's novels; it is deeper

and fuller, more glorious and more mean. One
must go to the greater novelists for the plummet
which sounds life's tragic depths, and for the
voices which repeat the music of the spheres. Even
the fairly comprehensive picture of the German
aristocracy which he essays to present requires
considerable modification to become a real mirror
of truth. However objective he may endeavour
to be, Ompteda is nevertheless an apologist for
his social class, and his stories have the inevitable
defects of all apologies. Luckily the material for
the correction of the picture is at hand in sufficient
amplitude, and we are in no danger of conceiving,
for example, the German army officer precisely
as Ompteda has painted him. Ompteda has no
divining rod for the discovery of hidden waters,
but he walks up and down in his little world, his
stately, old-fashioned garden, with keenly ob-
servant eyes; he is well acquainted with the traditional arrangement of the place, and would re-
gret to see the ancient growths uprooted and the
space given over to new and untried experiments;
but he is quite alive to the dangers which beset
all old-fashioned things, the choking weeds, the
deterioration of the soil, and the various processes of degeneration among the different species.
He is a cheerful and informing guide along those
pathways which he knows and loves.

THE GERMAN NOVEL AND THE
ETERNAL QUESTION

THE religion of dogma and ritual is a less insistent factor in the life and thought of Germany than it is in England and America. Hence the German novelist rarely presents the religious prepossessions of his characters as determinative in matters of conduct, even as the observance of ecclesiastical ordinances plays little part in the daily or weekly round. The established church is, to be sure, regarded as the handmaiden, or perhaps the morganatic wife of the state, and is honoured as such, primarily at weddings and funerals; the interposition of clergymen on such occasions constitutes a very considerable fraction of all references to church connections which one finds in German fiction. Many novelists, indeed, introduce clergymen as prominent characters, but they serve rather as recognized members of local society, available as dinner-guests, or as observers of life from the privileged aloofness of a secured living, than as religious experts, whose peculiar field is the eternal aspect of present conduct.

The religious dissensions of other days with their loosening of human passion obviously yield stirring material for historical fiction, as, for example, in the novels of Handel-Mazetti. Religious fanaticism in the peasant may lead to a pathetic type of exaltation and then to acts of misdirected heroism, as in Ganghofer's "Der

Dorfapostel" (The Village Apostle); and Clara
Viebig in "Das Kreuz im Venn" (The Cross in
Venn) seeks to show that religious beliefs and
practices may, in remote and unenlightened com-
munities, degenerate into superstitions which de-
grade and perhaps defile. In "Der geistliche Tod"
(Spiritual Death) Emil Mariott unfolds the grim
tragedy of a Roman priest in the throes of the
flesh, but the problem presented is a purely individual and human one; there are no dialectics on
the question of sacerdotal celibacy. After a
struggle of fitful years, several of Fontane's heroines seek the tranquillities of the Roman communion, but there are no doctrinal or controversial
elements in the motives for their flight; they
seek a lodgement for the troubled soul. But
novels dealing with present-day vagaries of religious belief, the ferment of critical and specu-
lative thinking, or with the martyrdoms of heter-
odoxy, have been less conspicuous in Germany
than in English-speaking lands. Polenz's "Der
Pfarrer von Breitendorf" (The Pastor at Breitendorf) and, much less significantly, the hero of
Kretzer's "Die Bergpredigt" (The Sermon on
the Mount) are perhaps the closest parallels to
our company of Robert Elsmeres and John
Wards.

Of late years, indeed, German consciousness of
incompetence and emptiness in the religion of the
churches has often found expression rather in
the cultivation of substitutes than in direct or
indirect criticism of the church itself. The vege-
tarians, the "Naturmenschen," the sunlight fana-

tics, the devotees of dress or marriage reform, have found a way of salvation without grace. Adherence to a cult, characterized by a system of beliefs or a theory of conduct, satisfies man's gregarious instincts and supplies the propulsive enthusiasm of the sects. These matters find their way into many novels; even the cult of nudity has its representative novel. In a more general way the efficiency of "Kultur" has been proposed as a substitute for the consolations of religion. The hero of Kretzer's novel makes express mention of this substitution and of its failure.

The novelists have not, however, forgotten entirely the question which was once put to the Pharisees, "What think ye of Christ?" Within a few years three eminent men of letters have faced this inquiry, and in the form of a novel they have pondered over the answer, Frenssen in "Hilligenlei," Rosegger in "I. N. R. I.," and Hauptmann in "Der Narr in Christo" (The Fool in Christ). Two of these novels contain a new version of the life of Christ, and the third may be interpreted as suggesting indirectly the general principles for such a revision of the gospel narrative. This is by no means a new phenomenon in the literature of Germany; a thousand years ago the life of Christ was retold in Old Saxon verse with such alterations as to adapt it to the prevailing taste; Christ appears as a splendid warrior and prince, the Galilean fishermen are His retainers. Indeed any effort of this sort implies modifications and readjustments to fit a changing world. The work of certain painters seeks a similar end through similar means. The primitive painters did, indeed,— somewhat like the early unknown poet,— paint naïvely erroneous versions of the gospel story, but the distortion was due to the real grandeur of their faith and to picturesque limitations imposed by their ignorance. But modern painters, such as von Uhde, Walther Firle, Gebhardt, have laboured with conscious art in depicting Christ in the midst of our everyday world, among the classes of society with whom He once walked. We are struck perhaps at first by the concrete presentation of an idea which is ordinarily only spiritually conceived, and yield to the emotional appeal. But upon second thought we resent this method of coaxing our imagination, and find the conceit shallow.

And ordinarily we experience a similar aversion to works of fiction which introduce the life · of Christ. It is quite too easy. The author is using material which is familiar to all, and is sacred to a larger part of his prospective readers. Then, further, whatever attitude supported by tradition or conviction we may assume toward the historicity of the gospels or toward their validity as a universal evangel, the story of Christ's life on earth involves a tragic situation which is absolutely unparalleled. That the Son of God should come down from His ineffable dwelling-place to live among men, and then, despised and rejected, should die to redeem them, is an incomparable conception. If we were to regard the gospel story as mere literature, it would be the supreme work of the human imagination. The author who em-

ploys this material as the chief or a subordinate
theme for his own narrative, seems to rely in
part upon other forces than his own creative abil-
ity. In such cases we subject the author's proofs
of sincerity to more than common scrutiny.

Of the three novelists just mentioned, Frenssen
alone answers the question as to our thought of
Christ with the assurance of a propagandist; he
not only answers it for himself, but with magis-
terial complacence he insists that his answer is
the only correct one. Frenssen's disapproval of
current orthodoxy was already indicated in "Jörn
Uhl"; the views of the local pastor who conceived
Christianity rather as a method of living than as
a many-articled dogma of faith, undoubtedly
coincided with Frenssen's own convictions. It is
Frenssen's purpose in "Hilligenlei" to state his
position more clearly and completely, and at the
same time to give it a critical basis. Out of the
ruined structure of Christian theology, he seeks
to select those solid building stones which have
resisted the disintegrating influences of time and
tempest. These are to be the foundation blocks
of his new temple.

By the bleak shore of the German Ocean, wind
swept, and battered by northern tempests, lies the
little town of Hilligenlei. A tradition lingers
among the simple folk that some day a man will
be born in Hilligenlei who shall make the country
actually a "holy land." To the rather slender
thread of this Messianic legend Frenssen attaches
the career of his hero. The story of this little
town is told with all the simplicity and charm

which made "Jörn Uhl" the best-loved book of a
decade. We meet the same stalwart men and
women of the northern shore, whose clear eyes
have never lost the wistful far-sight of the seafarers, who are schooled by the sea to a sense of
man's insignificance, and trained by adversity to
seek eternal foundations for human destiny. One
of the number, Kai Jans, the son of the schoolmaster, goes to a university, studies theology, and
becomes a Protestant pastor. He is troubled by
doubts born of the higher criticism, but he works
his way out to clarity of conviction, and embodies
his findings in a new life of Christ. This intercalated manuscript is quantitatively only a small
part of Frenssen's novel, but it is the part for
which the whole exists, it is the altar for the
shelter of which the building is constructed.

Frenssen's affirmed purpose is to present in
this narrative the achievements of German critical scholarship. He even appends a list of learned
authorities, the eminent German scholars of the
nineteenth century who have sought the truth, as
he says, with hesitation and holy awe; they have
sifted the pretensions of religious systems and
have discarded the chaff of superstition and stultifying tradition. In view of the transcending importance of his subject, there is an irritating nar-
rowness in Frenssen's exultant patriotism which
is parochial and out of place.

To trace in Frenssen's narrative the sources of
his divergences from the gospels, his omissions
and alterations, and to test their scholarly validity, would be the task of an authority in Biblical

criticism. He omits entirely the story of Bethlehem; he records Christ's boyhood visit to Jeru-
salem but discards the interview with the learned
doctors. In the preaching of St. John the Baptist,
he alters the message, omitting the call to repent-
ance, and emphasizes the national elements in his
conception of an approaching kingdom. The
temptation in the wilderness is expressed without
symbol, and consists simply in the lure of an
immediate and tangible success. The account of
the Last Supper is brief, and the command for
perpetual remembrance is deleted. Of the crucifixion Frenssen asserts that Christ uttered not a
word on the cross, that no friends or relatives
were with Him there, and that no one knows what
went on within His spirit.

Frenssen makes an evident effort to reconstruct
the story in such a way as to unburden it of its
traditional sanctity and inviolability. He realizes
that we react unconsciously to the remembered
holiness of once familiar words, however rigidly
logical we may be otherwise in the exercise of intellectual processes. Hence Frenssen omits almost
entirely the names of men and places. Joseph
and Mary are mentioned only once by name; only
a few times does he call individual disciples by
name,— only when any other kind of identification would be haphazard or cumbersome. Christ
Himself is usually called "the hero," with various
epithets, the most common of which is "simple"
or "unpretending;" the prophets are referred to
as the "heroes of old." The land of Palestine
is described, the village where Christ's youth is

spent, and the great city which is the lode-star
of the faithful, and there is reference to the
greater city far away which was the centre of the
world, but not one of these places is mentioned
by name. Similarly the novelist often changes
the wording of Christ's teachings, as he repeats
them, even the wording of the Lord's Prayer is
altered, unquestionably not through caprice, or
audacious effort at amendment, but simply to present material in unfamiliar form. The plan to
reduce the aloofness of the gospel story, to make
it more human and everyday, involves the use
of current terms in describing social and economic
conditions in Palestine; we hear of "foreign capital" and of "monopoly;" factional divisions in
political or religious thinking are supplied with
modern designations; references to the formu-
laries of Jewish ritual and priestly observance are
couched in terms which purposely suggest the
familiar liturgies and sacraments of Christian
worship. Great care is taken to account for the
background of misery and hopelessness, which
was fertile soil for the growth of the Messianic
belief.

Frenssen's chief concern, however, in his alterations in the narrative is to expunge the supernatural and the miraculous, or to reduce it to
inoffensive dimensions, and yet to retain for his
hero a dignity and exaltation combined with some
degree of authority. He must not appear merely
as a pitiful, self-deluded impostor. The miracles
of healing are apparently accepted as the work
of his "holy will to help and his proud certitude,"

coupled with resurgent faith on the part of the sick. But Frenssen is strangely hesitant and inconclusive even in the mere record of these happenings; he leaves us puzzled as to their reality. Is a physical change actually wrought, or is it simply a kind of hypnosis, a work of therapeutic suggestion, which banishes pain through the substitution of other and all-absorbing sensory experiences? The miracles of feeding are summarily disposed of, and in such a way as to suggest an interpretation for those of healing; the multitudes did not feel hunger and thirst. He made their souls so joyful and light that they forgot the body. This mesmeric power may be summoned to account for the conduct of the publican who rises from his seat and follows Christ simply at a look from the way-farer.

But the centre of Frenssen's whole problem is the relationship of his hero to a supernatural Messiahship. Here there is little satisfaction for the reader who seeks logical and orderly development from a beginning. In His boyhood Christ often stepped aside from the merry games of other children, as if listening to an invisible presence; in these moments a bright light burned within Him; He dreamed that the heavenly vision would soon be His. The familiar stories of the great hero whose coming had been foretold filled Him with ecstasy and awe. In baptism He is illumined with holy rapture in the conviction that the Eternal Power, the Father in Heaven, accepts "his glowing devotion and his pure will."

But in all this there is nothing to account for the Messianic consciousness of the hero, for an identification of himself with the one long-promised; this identification seems startling and contradictory when it is first presented. One is little aided by the curious and inept method which Frenssen employs here and elsewhere to suggest the development of an idea in the individual or the rise of tradition among a people. He records a series of ejaculatory expressions, varying in intensity or certainty; this betokens in the individual a process of self-scrutiny and indecision, tending to resolution; with the multitude it represents the indeterminate voices of the crowd, gradually accumulating conviction. The exclamations are accompanied by dots and dashes which are apparently intended to suggest endless repetition, variation, and increment. The presence of an idea in the mind of Christ is frequently developed in this manner; conviction is not acquired by a recorded process of reasoning. Belief in the non-rationalistic tenets of Christian creeds is accounted for in this naïve and novel way. In the very crises of his arguments Frenssen hides behind a row of dots.

And after Christ has gone, the story of His life is told and retold; the creative imagination, ever irrepressible and ever at the service of human need and human longing, adds new elements and new detail to its substance. And when He did not come again, as He had promised, a strong man arose and became His conservator, a man whose initial vision came in the form of an epileptic fit. Frenssen definitely diagnoses it thus. Upon the shoulders of St. Paul is laid the responsibility for the creation of the whole fabric of Christian dogma, whereby the simple Son of Man became the eternal and glorified Son of God. The accumulations of scholastic dogma down through the centuries are implied rather than described; but the whole tendency has been to obscure or falsify the original message. Even Luther's service, though Frenssen's patriotism seems reluctant to admit it, is characterized as still dissatisfying and incomplete, or essentially false. "In the last two centuries," Frenssen says, "the noblest of the people, the best poets, and all the wise and noble, young and old, turned away from this faith and this church." After so inclusive a generalization it seems odd that Frenssen should think it necessary to add a brief list of these apostates,—Frederick the Great, Goethe, and Helmholtz. Then, in a series of dithyrambic paragraphs at the end of the manuscript, Frenssen states the conclusions which he thinks are to be derived from his narrative. All traditional observances are rejected as neither pertinent nor authoritative, but as obsolete and befogging. The mass of tenets, canons, and creeds is discarded; of some of them it is said that those who believe in them are either ignorant or hypocritical. There remain two positive and irrefragable conceptions,—the goodness of an eternal power that holds us, and Christ as a figure of incomparable beauty, to whom this divine world-spirit has spoken its message of fatherly beneficence and its exhortation to brotherly love. This, Frenssen asserts, was his hero's creed; this is Christianity.

The sovereign fault in Frenssen's plan is either that he gives us the manuscript at all, or perhaps rather, that he attaches to it such a measure of significance. His hero's gospel was already being handed about in manuscript copies and was receiving attention, an intentional parallel to the early circulation of the gospel narratives; a further and more extended influence is promised through printing. Then, too, through the invention of the Hilligenlei legend Frenssen exalts his hero and his message; Kai Jans and his story are to be factors in a world-regeneration. But, after all, the narrative of Kai Jans is only Frenssen's personal interpretation, fortified by such scholarship as he considers authoritative; it is the gospel story with such omissions and alterations as suit a certain diligent and earnest student in the first decade of the twentieth century; it is not without charm, and though occasionally petty in its chauvinism, it is written with reverence. If a novelist insists that his heroine is a great singer or his hero a Paganini, we have no reason to dispute him. But when he invents a supremely great poet to be the hero of his novel, and then inserts some of his own verses as samples of his hero's work, the reality of the hero's eminence is immediately brought into question. The utterances of Fogazzaro's "Saint" seem less overwhelmingly significant than the author describes them; we wonder that the hearers are so moved. Frenssen's novel is shattered on the same rock, and in a much more disastrous fashion. We fail to regard the narrative as authentic or in any way infallible; it convinces us of nothing but Frenssen's sincerity.

Rosegger's life of Christ is also "set in a frame." The narrator is a criminal condemned to death, awaiting in his cell either the execution of the sentence or the arrival of a royal reprieve. His earlier life and the motive of his crime are only briefly suggested. Fernleitner is a simple carpenter who has reflected on the injustices of the social order and strayed into anarchistic brotherhoods. Then, haply the tool of the unscrupulous, the gentle-hearted workman attempted to assassinate the prime minister. Now in his imprisonment, old memories of childhood crowd upon him, and among them a dimly remembered story of divine forgiveness. The attendant monk, whose horizons are narrow though his heart is open wide, brings the prisoner a packet containing volumes of meditation and consolation; the gospel itself is not for the eyes of the uninitiated. The prisoner is not satisfied. He asks for pen and paper, and then, "as one who will wake himself at midnight before the Master comes," he begins to write his own life of Christ. For weeks he writes on, covering sheet after sheet. During the days of his imprisonment, his physical strength grows weak, he becomes the very shadow of a man. But in writing the gospel itself, this malefactor finds his way to paradise. The presiding judge of the court meets the monk coming from the cell; "You'll have a hard night of it," he says, "The criminal Fernleitner will need a priest. It's to-morrow at six o'clock." The pardon has been refused. But the priest replies that Fern-leitner no longer needed priest or judge. He had been pardoned by another King.

The situation which Rosegger thus conjures up is of great promise. Unfortunately he has realized but little of its possibilities. At the beginning he declines to cope with the inherent difficulty of style, and provides his artisan with a considerable taste in reading and a past habit of writing down his thoughts. This is a con-venience for Rosegger, but he forfeits a dis-tinctive merit of the design which he has conceived. An uneducated, or at least un-schooled, working-man, separated by years of wandering from the religious training of his childhood, might, when forced to unwonted contemplation and face to face with the ultimate things, write a gospel story which would stir our deepest selves. In it would mingle the shadowy remembrance of his mother's teachings, the naïve faith of childhood, soiled by thoughtless and perhaps wanton years, and the myopic wis-dom of personal experience. The evangel thus re-created and unconsciously adapted to the sinner's view of life would be a kind of "Caliban on Setebos," in its very artlessness being the more perfect revelation of the sinner's soul.

Rosegger also yields to the temptation of the story-teller; he obscures the simplicity of the "plot" by a web of coincidences, combinations, and additions. On the journey to Egypt the fugitives are attacked by two Bedouin robbers who convey them to their cavern. One of these robbers, Barab, is apparently a pupil of Nietzsche; to him strength is the only virtue, and extermination of the weak is the only charity. Later in the evening the robbers throw dice for the booty, but when the mother is the prize in question, the dice turn up without spots. Later still, in the darkness of night, the younger robber, Dismas, is moved to compassion, and while Barab sleeps, he leads the little family to safety. The temptation in the wilderness involves a second meeting with the robber Barab, he is the head of a large company of Bedouins, and Christ is tempted to use this power for worldly ends. The "rich young man" is troubled by the consciousness that wealth and pleasure are impermanent; he hears that a prophet in the wilderness has the gift of eternal life and imperishable possessions, and he seeks him, only to receive the disconcerting admonition. On his way back, he encounters Barab, King of the Desert; his riches are taken from him, and he tries to bargain for life itself. An expedition headed by the zealot Saul captures both robbers, and they are the malefactors of the crucifixion; Dismas is the thief to whom the promise of paradise is given. And the "rich young man" is the Simon who bears the cross; he had freed his slaves, dismissed his women, given away the superfluity of his possessions, but was still unsatisfied; now amid the jeers of the multitude he bears the sign of infamy, and is filled with inexpressible joy.

Akin to this arrangement of plot is the repeated use of foreshadowing devices. As Joseph and Mary journey to Bethlehem, Mary wavers and sinks by the wayside. Nearby a man is nailing two wooden beams together. "The one who is to use it doesn't want it," is his cryptic reply to Joseph's question concerning the crossed beams. Mary is pierced by a mysterious terror, and they hasten on toward Bethlehem. In His boyhood Christ worked in the carpenter's shop at Nazareth; one day as He is busy fitting a door frame together, unconsciously, half in dream, He places two beams cross-wise over one another, while the words "He was numbered with the transgressors" ring in His ears. This conceit is a version of the familiar "Shadow of the Cross." These easy arrangements of plot and characters, this use of foreboding hints, may seem artificial or impressive according to the predisposition of the reader.

The most successful of Rosegger's additions to the narrative are the occasional touches of homely detail or playful humour. They humanize the story without degrading it. Joseph appeals to a fruit vendor in Bethlehem for a night's lodging, explaining the reason for their presence there and stating their descent from David; "Well, you've descended a good way" is the remark of the wag. According to this gospel story, the Holy Family remained twelve years in Egypt;

on the journey back Mary is busy with mending,
for they must not arrive in their former home
too shabbily clad. One relative in Nazareth views
the arrival of the wanderers with considerable
concern, for he has established himself in the
carpenter's shop, and at first declines to be dis-
placed. But Joseph was of an orderly mind; he
proves his ownership of the tools left there
years before by pointing to the "J" marked on
them. Judith, the wife of Levi-Matthew, re-
bukes her husband for his niggardliness; she
wants a Greek cloak such as "Rebecca and
Amala wear." But it is a cruel fancy to send a
pedlar about among the crowd offering the seam-
less robe for sale.

Of what might be the most interesting aspect
of his theme, Rosegger makes little use; he introduces only hesitatingly the possible contrasts
and reconciliations between the prisoner's socialistic or anarchistic ideas and the gospel which
he is narrating. The conflict between rich and
poor, capital and labour, is indeed touched upon,
but there is little made of it. The parables are
often discussed and interpreted by the disciples.
This was Rosegger's great opportunity. There
is, however, no controversy on the parable of
workers in the vineyard who receive an equal
wage though some have borne the burden and
heat of the day and others have worked only
toward eventide. It is simply taken as the
promise of a welcome for late-comers to the
Kingdom. The listeners shake their heads over
the story of the king who invites men "from the

high-ways and hedges" to the wedding feast, and yet excludes one who appears without a wedding garment; "he ought to know beforehand," says one of the disciples, "that people of the streets have no wedding garments." The parable of the unjust steward raises questions. A muleteer gives an explanation which apparently receives the Master's commendation: "No one of us has any property on earth; we are all only the stewards of our possessions, and when we give to the needy, we are indeed unjust stewards, because we have given what is not ours, but we are nevertheless doing right." To the "rich young man," one of the disciples gives an explanation of his Master's words which is a strangely frank acceptation of a non-socialistic principle. Every one should have as much property as he individually needs. Simon's position is aristocratic, and he needs wealth to maintain it; the very process of maintaining it gives employment to many; this is economically a great benefit to the country. Danger lurks merely in excess of possessions beyond one's needs. One disciple, indeed, insists that the wealth which employees create in the fields, the mines, and the workshops does not really belong to the rich, and a new parable is invented to symbolize the interdependence of all workers. One aspect of the miracles of healing is characteristically emphasized; the lame beggars are deprived of the very tools of their idleness and are sent home to work. The circumstances in which this gospel story is written doubtless ac-

count for the prisoner's explanation of Judas's
betrayal; Judas is a devoted disciple, but he does
not understand his Master; he is confident that
Christ can destroy his enemies by thunderbolts
from Heaven, and broodingly he resolves to
force his Lord to act, the only way to redeem
a lost cause. The kiss itself is accompanied by
the thought: "Messiah King, now reveal Thy-
self!" In another passage Fernleitner seems to
take upon himself the sin of Cain, who slew his
brother.

As Frenssen's gospel aims at a universal application, the chief merit of Rosegger's plan lies
in its personal and individual aspects. Frenssen
writes with the conviction that unassailable
scholarship substantiates his pronouncements;
Rosegger knows nothing of the higher criticism;
his prisoner has not even a text for comparison.
If Frenssen avoids the names of men and places,
Rosegger delights in them, he invents names for
characters in the gospel narrative which are
nameless there, and manufactures new characters
to fill his picture. Frenssen eschews the marvellous; he desires to humanize the superhuman,
his supreme conclusion is that his hero was a
man like other men, and he is petulantly irritated
at any suggestion of Mariolatry. Rosegger allows the miraculous to play havoc with rational
experience; his story begins and ends in wonder.
Frenssen simplifies and rationalizes, whilst Rosegger embroiders and sentimentalizes.

Hauptmann's novel "Der Narr in Christo;
Emanuel Quint" is a very different kind of book.

The hero doubtless bears a resemblance to Dostoievsky's "Idiot." Like him, Emanuel Quint lacks the human trait of self-seeking, but in a much more positive way, for he is possessed with a veritable passion of self-effacing love. We are confronted with the same baffling mystery, quite unsolved, if we seek sources for the negative and positive qualities which separate this selfless one from his fellowmen. Hauptmann causes his story to develop into a kind of Messiad. It is, in its essence, the simple and pathetic tale of a Silesian peasant who tries to walk in the footsteps of Christ, and then, through a combination of strange vicissitudes, loses his mental balance and confuses his own identity with that of his Master.

The narrative begins somewhat abruptly with Emanuel's first public appearance as the messenger of a coming kingdom. From this first sermon on to his death, there is much in Emanuel's life which agrees with the events as narrated in the gospels. Disciples join him, mostly from the poor and ignorant, some of them leave all to follow him. He is baptized in a stream by a fanatical Moravian brother. He wanders in the wilderness and is tempted. He visits the distressed, and the sick are brought to him. Children come to him, and he speaks to them of the kingdom. Clergymen of the established church reason with him and are astonished at his doctrine. A rich young man seeks him, questioning as to the worth of life. He is reviled and persecuted, is jeered at and spat upon. He is arrested as a vagrant and a seditious agitator, and the judge does not know what to do with him. He goes up to Breslau, the capital city, and there is a Judas who betrays him. He is charged with a crime of which he is guiltless, yet he opens not his mouth.

Often the parallel becomes vague and inconclusive, and there is much in the story which no ingenuity can make analagous to the scriptural narrative. After his first arrest and release, Emanuel is brought back to the little village which has been his home—where he had been a rather indifferent worker in the carpenter's shop of his step-father. But the stir which he has made in the country-side soon tears him from this seclusion; his disciples seek him out, but he begs them to go home and try to lead the life of Christ, each in his own normal tasks. For a time Emanuel finds a patroness in the "Guhrauer Fräulein," a pious lady of aristocratic birth and great riches. He lives on her estate in the house of the head gardener. Over the gardener's daughter Emanuel exercises a strange mesmeric influence. Ruth Heidebrand is a high-strung, abnormal child, a dreamer of other worlds; she had already fallen once into a "magnetic" or cataleptic sleep, and another comes upon her during Emanuel's stay. In her relationship to the visitor there is a mingling of reverence, worship, and purely human love. With reticence Hauptmann suggests characteristics of adolescence governing her ecstatic, religious emotionalism. The relationship of Hannele to the

schoolmaster, which the drama "Hanneles Himmelfahrt" betrays dimly through fevered visions,
is here worked out in sharper outlines; it is more
directly conceived as a psychological and pathological state.

Out of this secure retreat Emanuel is rudely
dragged. Some of his disciples have founded a
communistic religious settlement, "the brothers
of the valley," and live together in a mill. With
them a primitive religious fervour is now exposed
to the influence of comparative physical idleness
and the constant stimulus of inflaming companionships. Revels and orgies result, in which bodily
contortions are the expression of spiritual exaltation, and the carnal instincts lurk in ambuscade.
They ponder over Emanuel's teachings; their
childish curiosity is particularly teased by his oft-
recurrent phrase, "the mystery of the Kingdom,"
and they dispatch a messenger to him, in order
that they may share in his mystery. Emanuel is
shocked and angered by what he hears of his
disciples, and he goes to them at once. He forces
the brothers to disband, but by the very might
of his personality, in the inexplicable authority
which he exercises over them, he binds them all
anew to him in love, devotion, and even worship.
But, before the dispersal of the community,
Emanuel is forced to face a personal problem
which was capable of nullifying his mission. Ruth
Heidebrand runs away from home and finds
her way to Emanuel. He resists the temptation
of her love and brings her back to her parents.
Though her father comes to realize Emanuel's

innocence, the excited temper of the region bars Emanuel from a return to the quiet asylum. Again his disciples seek him, and he goes forth with them, to Breslau, where he establishes himself in a squalid little tavern, and sends out messengers of his gospel. They do not preach to deaf ears, and new phases of his influence develop in the new environment.

But lines are laid for a tragic disruption of his activity. Bohemian Joseph was one of Emanuel's earliest disciples, a monkey-faced border smuggler, and a thief of considerable notoriety. A superstitious spell binds him to the apostle, and when once this spell is broken, the devil awakens within him. He lures little Ruth from her home to Breslau by means of a crude letter written in Emanuel's name, and then murders her. In the garden of an inn outside the city, Emanuel washes the feet of his disciples after meat. At the first drop of water, Joseph starts up in terror and rushes from the little company, the stain of Judas is already upon him. Even now the officers of the law are seeking Emanuel as the murderer. He even confesses the crime, and makes no attempt to defend himself. But the truth is later revealed; Joseph has hanged himself on the spot where the deed was done. Emanuel is released; he wanders over Germany, goes into Switzerland, and disappears. In the spring when the snows melt, a body is found on the St. Gotthard Pass which is recognized as that of the unhappy prophet.

The external events which make up the "plot" of the story, Hauptmann has constructed with great skill; there is a logical precision in the sequence of events, there is a unity of impression, a relevancy to ultimate purpose in the selective accumulation from possible happenings, which betokens epic power of a high order. Hauptmann's training in dramatic writing has given him also a plastic skill in presenting character vividly and completely within narrow limits; he imparts a fine semblance of life and reality to the individual disciples, the country folk, the wretched weavers in their filthy warrens, the country society of clergy and squirearchy, or the Bohemian dregs of a large city. But the main theme of the story is a spiritual one; it lies within the mind of Emanuel Quint.

As with Frenssen, the growth of the Messianic consciousness in his hero is to Hauptmann a vexatious stumbling-block; but he faces his problem much more honestly. His task, one may readily admit, is a far easier one. At the beginning Emanuel insists that he is not the Christ, that he is merely one of many sent to heal the broken-hearted, only a man, the son of man,— and then he is startled and terrified when he realizes that he has thus used his Master's designation of Himself. But on reflection he decides that this is not an unwarranted presumption, for he lives Christ, walks in His steps, and is inspired by a transcending love. So he consents somewhat reluctantly to a kind of homage; his disciples kiss his hands; the wretched, who seek his aid, bow down before him. His over-mastering love shrinks from disillusioning them, from shattering the pitifulness of their faith. Naturally the effort to imitate Christ, to re-produce the life of Christ in himself, leads Emanuel to invite experiences which correspond to the gospel story.

During the night of his first imprisonment, Emanuel has a dream of Christ; the vision is more actual to him than many of the attested happenings of waking hours. From that moment on, the transfusion of identity gradually becomes to him an established verity. When the wayworn disciples find him after a separation, he seeks un-consciously a reconciliation between their adora-tion and his own conviction of his re-birth, of God in him. The more he talks to them, the more he involves himself and them in the conception of a heavenly likeness, merging into an identity. "There is only one Christian," he says, "and that is Christ, to be a Christian is the same as being Christ, that is, having Christ in you." From this insidious identification of himself with the his-torical Christ follows the later repudiation of prayer. Why should he pray to himself? The Bible is also discarded; it is the work of erring men; the errors of centuries involving the wretchedness of generations are built upon it. Among the blasphemies which the authorities lodged against Emanuel was his violent treat-ment of the sacred book. He throws it angrily and irreverently across the room, the very tat-tered little volume out of which his youth had

drawn its faith.   In the last period of Emanuel's
ministry his love for suffering and deluded humanity is touched with a strange exultant assurance and mingled with occasional outbursts of
indignation against the rulers of the world,
temporal and ecclesiastical; and in a kind of
apocalyptic vision, he prophesies their passing
from the earth.

The assumption of Messiahship is a familiar
phenomenon of mental unbalance.   Throughout
the Christian era, eager apostles have wearied at
the tarrying of their Lord, and on the borderland
between conscious volition and hysteria, they have
surrendered themselves to the fateful presumption.   On a lowlier level stand the numberless
"Christs" whose pitiful delusions sadden the annals of the asylums.   Hauptmann is plainly at a
loss where to classify his "fool."   Emanuel's life
brings him into association with many kinds of
people; he is a puzzle to most of them,—and he
remains a puzzle even to his own creator.   To
the Moravian brother, an itinerant evangelist,
who combines religious fanaticism very shrewdly
with a practical discernment, Emanuel appears as
an enigma.   When the evangelist first sees him,
the words come to his mind: "Surely he hath
borne our griefs and carried our sorrows."   This
unnamed stranger is to him a figure of mystery
and awe.   The physician in the insane asylum
can make nothing out of him, though a kind of
scientific label has to be attached to him.   The
jealous lover of Ruth Heidebrand is fresh from
the materialistic scepticism of his medical studies,

but his incredulity yields to curiosity and perplexity. His ready psychiatric diagnosis falls
short of conviction. The "Guhrauer Fräulein"
visits him in the hospital. As an erring though
earnest seeker after divine truth, he is the object
of her real interest as well as of her largesse.
But she is dumb-founded at the effect of his
presence on her inner life. Though she rejects
Emanuel's Messianic presumption, there has been
produced within her a strange illusion of the
Saviour's nearness. Two youthful radicals from
Berlin, superbly confident in their recently acquired equipment of modern notions, encounter
Emanuel, while they are taking a walking trip
among the Silesian mountains. They regard him
as a specimen of extraordinary interest, and take
notes of his peculiarities for the books with which
they are going to startle the world. But they
rub their eyes in mystification when he has gone
from them.

In spite of the warning of the bee-keeper,
Emanuel handles the bees carelessly and fear-
lessly, he plucks them from his clothing, from his
beard. Crowds gather by the wayside and jeer
at Emanuel as a police officer accompanies him
home after his first arrest. But a little boy steals
out from the company and tries to thrust a piece
of bread into Emanuel's pocket, and is dismayed
that his charity is observed. But somehow after
this, jeering ceases to seem a worthy pastime. In
Breslau countless numbers of people come to the
apostle, not merely the ignorant and the outcast, but baronesses and countesses, military men,

and many a person of prominence. They do not shun the unsavoury spot; they wait in the ugly, unkempt tavern room as in an ante-chamber, those ordinarily haughty and arrogant are shy and humble, and they tell Emanuel of their secret woe. And Emanuel's answer to them all is only a re-wording, or fresh application of the Sermon on the Mount. Why did they come?

After his release from prison, Emanuel wanders far and wide about Germany; he knocks at hundreds of doors, asking for lodging and for bread, and answering the question as to his identity with the name of the Redeemer. "Involuntarily one thanks Heaven that the wanderer was only a poor fool of earth and not Christ Himself, for otherwise, hundreds of Catholic and Protestant clergymen, workmen, officials, judges, merchants, presiding elders, bishops, nobles and burghers, in short, numberless pious Christians would have ladened themselves with the curse of damnation. . . . But how could one know whether it was not the real Saviour after all, who, in the disguise of a poor fool, wanted to see how far the seed sown by God, the seed of the Kingdom, had grown toward the harvest?" In the pocket of the dead man a bit of paper was found, bearing the familiar legend "The mystery of the kingdom." "Did he die still convinced or doubting? . . . The paper contains a question surely, but what does it mean, the mystery of the Kingdom?"

Thus Hauptmann closes his narrative with an interrogation point. He has ended the story in

his own bewilderment; he has conjured up a
fictitious tale which grips him; it embodies an
idea which has held him from boyhood and will
not let him go. In the early days of his literary
apprenticeship, directly after the sensational
flourish of his first drama, Hauptmann wrote a
little sketch called "Der Apostel," which contained the germ of "The Fool in Christ." The
hero is a religious fanatic who thinks himself the
messenger of a new gospel, a new Christ; his
gospel is a world of peace, or rather peace for
the world, peace in all the relations between man
and man. "Nature" is the gateway to this more
perfect world. At the root of the story lies the
same fundamental human mystery as in "The
Fool in Christ." Is there a sentient power which
enfolds us, giving now and then to chosen spirits,
—who then seem abnormal in this duller world,
—their visions of human perfectibility? This is
the question which puzzles and baffles. Hauptmann tries to reason it out, perhaps to reason it
away. But he can not get away from the problem
which he can not solve.

In telling the story of Emanuel Quint, Hauptmann makes use of a familiar method of indirect
narration; he pretends that he is simply presenting the record of a chronicler who, interested in
the reported phenomena of the apostle's life, has
taken upon himself to investigate, to accumulate
material, and then set it in an orderly narrative.
If Hauptmann intended to tell the story through
the medium of another personality, adding to its
interest through the creation of a narrator in

whose mind it is reflected, his purpose has signally failed. The reader is in no way aware of the personality of the chronicler, is only at rare intervals even reminded of the device of an intermediary narrator; and, as a matter of fact, Hauptmann himself seems to recall it only now and then, generally narrating, with the conceded omniscience of the novelist, matters which no chronicler, however minute his investigations, could ever have found out. The fiction of the chronicler is after all a rather transparent device; Hauptmann uses it as a cloak for his own uncertainty, but contrariwise perhaps, it merely uncovers more plainly his attitude of perplexity in the presence of the mystery.

The religious life of every country presents an intricate pattern. In no other field of our thinking is there so admirable an attestation of the adage which attributes to a given number of men an equal number of opinions. It would seem as if intellectual sloth were the only champion of uniformity. The pattern shifts, too, even while we try to trace it; its lines become as involved and as unstable as the wave-lines of a ruffled sea. The irruption of a commanding personality disturbs the design; external events or temporary conditions, such as war, and peace, prosperity, and adversity, may underscore or blur the fundamental features of the pattern.

Hence it can not be said that these novels cover all the varieties of religious experience in Germany, or that the attitude toward ancient faiths represented by any one of them, even if momentarily predominant, is necessarily likely to remain so. These stories obviously do not account for the goodly number of people who have no religious opinions at all worth mentioning. There are those who think intelligently, objectively, and comprehensively, and find their only answer in absolute disbelief, which may or may not coincide with their desires. There are those who think they think and come to the same conclusion. And there is the vast mass of those who learn by rote and then repeat and act by rote, as it were, on demand, simply as a matter of good form or thoughtless habit, and make no pretence of thinking at all. But these novels do nevertheless represent three conspicuous classes of serious-minded men, who are seriously concerned about their relationship to the fabric of Christian thought and principle, about the survival in themselves and society of a seemingly ineradicable presence.

Frenssen reasserts the Christian faith as the hope of the world. But he holds that its vitality is threatened by a cancerous growth, the accretion of centuries; the time has come for a rigid policy of rejection and retention, though he compromises sufficiently to allow to some of these unfounded accessories the possibility of a temporary practical value. And Frenssen insists that the residue, after he has performed the task of rejection, is not a new Christianity, but the only real Christianity that has ever existed. He exults over his achievement; it is his conviction that this new old gospel can still redeem mankind. Frens-

sen is merely one of many professional and lay
thinkers, who have accepted the burden of revitalizing religious faith through a process of
extreme simplification.

Rosegger has elsewhere expressed his own religious ideas even more completely and definitely
than in this novel, notably in the volume which
he calls "Mein Himmelreich" (My Kingdom of
Heaven). But the story of the condemned
criminal is indubitably a concrete expression of
his own beliefs. Rosegger doubtless enjoyed the
digressions of his criminal hero in his effort to
recall and reproduce the story of Christ's life,
for he is a story-teller by profession, but these
digressions are held in suspension, as it were, and
are not coalescent; they have no effect whatever
on the essentials of the narrative. The dogma of
the redemption is the foundation of the story
and it is accepted in its entirety. In his various
utterances on religious matters, Rosegger betrays
occasionally an alien reflection and questioning;
at times upon the surface of his traditional confession there appears a tinge of mystic pantheism.
But at heart he is still unflinchingly orthodox; he
is at heart still a peasant, and his religion is the
orthodoxy of the peasant.

Hauptmann's "Fool in Christ" is neither a
denial nor an affirmation. Even if we were to
force the parallelism, the novelist does not by
implication either dispute or confirm the essential events of the gospel narrative or the
elements of Christian dogma. He ponders over
man and God,—man in his infinite pettiness

reaching out to lay hold on Infinite Greatness. In early life the novelist, like all his fellows, learned a story which made this process simple and concrete. Is it still a valid gospel which holds life and more than life here and hereafter? Naturally the novelist observes his own peculiar method of seeking and testing truth, but his query, his search of the Scriptures for their testimony, characterizes unnumbered hosts of his contemporaries. In plaintive undertone, they echo the Psalmist's cry "Oh, that I knew where I might find Him!" So Hauptmann's book is a characteristic record of present-day seeking after God. It is contemplative, quizzical perhaps, and hauntingly pathetic. Hauptmann has many companions in this wistful bewilderment.

ERNST ZAHN: SWISS NOVELIST

THE Swiss are primarily engaged in entertaining guests from all the world; they share with us the sublimity of their scenery and provide for our material wants with generosity and intelligence. But our real acquaintance with them is all the more meagre because their knowledge of our needs makes possible for them an almost silent service. To most travellers the Swiss people and their habitations are simply incidental to the scenery. The Swiss herdsman on the mountain heights seems a picturesque ornament to the landscape; men and women make hay on upland slopes, and we see them at their work; they eat their noon-day meal, looking indifferently at passing diligence or chance pedestrian; they sit by the roadside to sell us edelweiss, or paper-knives, or hat-pins made of glacial pebbles. The doors and windows of their cottages are often wide open for our curiosity, the little intimacies of their domesticity seemingly revealed; they are so much in evidence, yet so little known. It is, perhaps, difficult to think of them as leading a complex life of their own apart from their conscious or unconscious function of serving us. But the novelist may become a revealer and interpreter.

The novels of Ernst Zahn have as a background only a very restricted portion even of this tiny land, either within a day's tramp from his home at Göschenen on the St. Gotthard Pass,

195

or in the town of St. Felix, which is his name
for Zürich, or by the lake on which it lies. In
his few attempts at historical fiction the horizon
is not pushed farther back. But within very confined geographical boundaries the mirror of the
whole world may be found.

To establish a connection between the characteristics of a people and the climatic and topo-
graphical features of the territory which they
inhabit is an alluring, often too alluring, solution
of recognized differences. Within limits, however, the validity of such an inference is unassailable. A life lived against a natural background
of stern unfriendliness develops different human
traits from those produced in kindlier regions;
the sustenance of life is wrested from grim,
unyielding forces of nature; in the other case
nature is a lavish giver. Thus similar characteristics may be predicated of mountain folk
and of those who live by northern seas; in both
cases a rugged race is developed, capable of passion, but habituated to self-control. The inner
life is nourished, but habits of repression prevent
manifestation of it. All the more perilous then
is the flood of passion when once the barriers are
broken down. There is, however, a distinction
between the mountains and'the sea; the mountains
are vast, uncompromising, brutal, the sea is infinite, capricious, cruel; but the mountains enforce
isolation and loneliness, they are world barriers;
the sea is relatively sociable, it is the pathway of
world intercourse. Pent up within their rocky
walls, the mountaineers are lonelier and narrower

than the seafarers; they are more monosyllabic in their utterance, more rigid, more inexorable in their conduct of life. They are less resourceful, more given to a sullen resignation in defeat; and they are outwardly more devout.

An individual and interesting type of womanhood is developed under such standards of living. One of the most familiar figures in Zahn's stories is the masterful, austere woman of middle life, with whom there is no outward proof of emotional experience, yet a rigid conformity to religious observances. Such a heroine is Clari-Marie. Though trained for one service, to usher children into the world, Clari-Marie fills acceptably the position of country doctor in the mountain hamlet of Isengrund; she is also a kind of general counseller, or, indeed, dictator in the affairs of the whole community, which she holds in unconscious subjection to the might of her personality. She works too in the cabinet-maker's shop, and with the strength of a man; this had been the trade of her worthless, drunken husband. At home she is the controlling factor in all the household concerns. The care of the old people is hers; wee bundles of rags, who sit all day in the chimney corner with a refrain of constant lament on their withered lips. The other members of the family are a younger sister, now approaching middle age, gaunt, haggard, and silent, slip-shod in body and mind, and her boy Juan, whose very presence is a reminder of vanished youth and sullied honour.

One by one Clari-Marie's cares forsake her, find substitutes, or leave voids worse than the cares themselves. The old people die. Juan, weak, bloodless, physically incapable of earning his living in mountain ways, is educated by chance friends down in the valley. Clari-Marie regards the populous lowlands as the abode of lax morals and frivolous views of life, and she opposes his going. She really loves the lad and dreads the loneliness of his absence, but when he goes, she merely shakes hands with him as if he were going to a neighbour's house for the afternoon. Clari-Marie goes then far up the mountains to the valley where a married sister lives in pinched and acrimonious poverty; she suggests that the two children, Hansi and Severina, should come to the house for dinner when they are in the village on school days. In no way does she hint that it is only her yearning for the companionship of her kindred. Juan returns, a skilled physician, and after a time sets up his own house. To it his mother goes, but without a word to Clari-Marie. Rigidly the silent woman goes about her tasks, still further embittered that the villagers turn gradually and secretly from her and seek the advice of her nephew. Clari-Marie's relentless orthodoxy is wounded by Hansi's marriage to one outside the fold, and Severina dies because Juan had not been called in time. Though at the trial Clari-Marie frees them from the formal charges, there is a persistent suspicion that the showy piety of her sister and brother-in-law covers a hideous sin. She is gradually losing confi-

dence in herself and her prepossessions concerning
life; all her plans, all her theories fail. At last the
ageing woman turns her back on the village and
goes up the farther heights to Hansi's home, perhaps to learn love and the way of its expression;
—"Perhaps,—there lies gold in earth's depths
where never a miner finds it; and there are men
and women, strong, hard, and reserved, whose
inner life can not give up its gold, because the
soul lives in a shell as hard as the bitter, unfruit-
ful bosom of earth." "Clari-Marie" is the
tragedy of those whom temperamental and intellectual rigidity condemn to embittered loneliness.

The heroine of the little story "Die Mutter"
(The Mother) is of the same austere, rigid sort.
With reminiscent tenderness of motherhood un-
spoken, she prepares the bed for her son when
word comes that the wanderer is to return after
years in America; with intuitive misgivings she
divines the weakness of his character, and in the
following days her tearless eyes have penetrated
his utter worthlessness. Then to save him from
a deed of nameless infamy, she takes the life of
him, her son. The judges who have condemned
her to a year in prison stand with bared heads
as she is led by. The days pass till her release.
In her simple black gown, the kerchief laid over
her head, her strong hands crossed under her
breast, she walks home. People meeting her
start back and look aside in order not to greet
her, but her sunken cheeks do not blush; she is
not troubled any more by her fellow creatures,
in the months of imprisonment she has settled

her account with her God. She steps into the
cottage as if she were returning from a brief
walk. "What are you making to-day?" she asks
as she enters the kitchen, and then picking up
the spoon which her startled granddaughter has
dropped, she begins to stir in the pan with it.
Thus she enters again into the world of everyday as if she had never forsaken it. Haggard,
pallid, dour, she sits with her memories. "The
women of that land can not really weep; they
have neither words nor gestures nor groans for
that which tortures them."

Similar too is the patrician mother of the hero
in "Einsamkeit" (Solitude), though in a very
different sphere of life. Steel yourself to be dependent on no one; have no friends, then you will
not be disappointed in them; the only way to
peace is to hold yourself at a distance from other
people. She has the poise and intelligence to
formulate in some such way as this her scheme
of life, but her barren peace is marred because
she cannot apply her theories of indifference to
her only son.

Zahn's stories are rarely dramatic in concentration. The novelist who leans to the dramatic
produces a closely wrought narrative of entangle-
ment, with manipulation of incident, leading to
a conclusion where the matters involved become
static; this supplies the idea of "end," and the
nature of their suggested permanence affords the
familiar designations of a "happy" or "unhappy"
ending. Sometimes indeed Zahn avails himself
of happenings, perhaps rather forcedly intro-

duced, in order to turn abruptly the current of men's lives according to his plans. But often with finer insight he allows time to be the chief determining element, as it is in life. Most of Zahn's longer tales and even many of the shorter ones cover many years, or take emphatically into account the simple influence of the ageing process on the very substance of our life. Zahn does not believe in the determinative power of episodical experience.

In "Herrgottsfäden" (Threads of God's Weaving), the story recounts the fortunes of two successive generations. At the beginning, a passion, elemental, torrential, sweeps two young people on, Rosi, the daughter of Felix Furrer, the local magistrate, and Christian Russi, handsome and headstrong, but only a workman in her father's service. It is the old story of youth and moonlight. Irate and obdurate, Furrer uses the power of his position and wealth not only to forbid so senseless a marriage but with violence he forces Christian and his mother to leave the community. To cloak Rosi's fault, he provides a husband out of his kinsfolk, a submissive nonentity, but the child which is born he utterly refuses to see. Years pass. Rosi is withered and ageing, heavy lines mar her forehead, and a certain shyness, a heaviness, have taken possession of her; she is not soured, but timid and phlegmatic. She finds a kind of listless joy in her two boys, Tobias, called by the villagers "the secret one" because of the effort to keep him from his grandfather's

sight, and Felix born some years after her marriage. And then Christian comes back out of
the unknown, a widower with three daughters;
in the midst of a business activity which has
spelled a considerable success, there has been in
his consciousness the thought that some day he
would come back and show his worth, perhaps
to the discomfiture of his old foe. But the passions of youth have been conquered by work; joy
in work for its own sake has dimmed the thought
of vengeance. Other forces have entered into
his life and shaped it whether he would or no.
And his return is in accordance with business
plans long cherished, though the purpose which
prompted them no longer masters him. The
second part of the story turns to the younger
generation and its sinister relationship to the
happenings of other days.

The years play their part in "Verena Stadler."
From Herrlibach on the lake Verena comes to
St. Felix to live with her relative, Frau Waser,
lately widowed. Verena is young and good-look-
ing. She captures the heart of the widow and
proves a capable helper in house and bake-shop,
lifting burdens from bowed shoulders. To the
widow's son her eyes turn; Wilhelm is almost
a giant in size and strength, gentle to his mother,
and good-humoured to all, but morally spineless.
His nature is as yet untouched by romance, but
one day on the lake there is a half conscious out-
burst of boyish affection which she takes for love;
this is her golden day. Later Wilhelm yields to
his mother's wishes, particularly when hopeless

illness comes upon her, and the engagement is announced. But Wilhelm falls under the spell of a pretty face, breaks his engagement, and brings into the house the teary, well-meaning Hilde, whom the mother, now bed-ridden, refuses to see. Verena stays on; she can not leave the old lady in her illness and trouble, and when death relieves her of this charge, Verena stays to care for weak, clinging Hilde, and when Hilde dies, to care for Hilde's child. The test of life is always there; she stands beside the man she loves, knowing that only her care keeps the affairs of house and shop from ruin, knowing without false pride that she has the power to keep him from evil, to shield him from the disintegrating forces which beset him, and yet this power she can not exercise. Then Wilhelm proposes, and Verena accepts. Neither of them is young any more; her girlish slenderness has changed to leanness, lines are graven on her face, her hands are rough and misshapen from work; there is something severe and angular about her. Wilhelm has changed too; there are shadows under his eyes and his hair has thinned, the good humour of other days has become an indolent indifference, a slackness of thought and action, a staring, brooding dulness. There is no shred of romance on his side, only a despairing self-seeking, and with her there is but the rugged path of duty, tinged with the glow of a dead dream. But Wilhelm's character is too disordered for her strength, and she cannot keep him permanently from the course of conduct which brings him to his end. Verena lives on, devoting herself to the other woman's child.

The conditions of married life are particularly susceptible to the influence of passing years. Husband and wife may grow strangers to one another as in "Der Liberi," and a word of old-time tenderness or even a suggestion of interest or concern may be merely an irritating reminder of a disillusioning process. In "Menschen" (Men and Women) and "Die Gerechtigkeit der Marianne Denier" (The Rectitude of Marianne Denier) the problem is that of a marriage in which one remains strong and healthy while the other is hopelessly invalided, a wreck of human-kind. The theme of "Die Rechnung des Josef Infanger" (Josef Infanger's Calculation) is the same, save that the physical disparity was present at the beginning.

At first thought, the material of Zahn's novels and the general angle from which the novelist approaches it might seem to make for a disabling monotony, the monotony of that song which has only one note, sung with varied stress and provided with an artfully deceiving accompaniment. It is true that most of his characters are humble folk, leading very humble and even humdrum lives. The great world of high finance and polit-ical or social ambitions, modern organizational effort for crippling human life or redeeming it, are but dim rumours in the mountain valleys. Yet within the limitations of experience to which his people are subjected Zahn finds the essential in all human experience; the relationships be-

tween man and man, the compelling convictions
and emotions. Zahn's themes are elemental, or
primitive perhaps; some of them indeed are
somewhat unusual. Lukas Hochstrasser takes
into his house the girl whom his scapegrace son
has ruined, and then after a time falls in love
with her himself, though he dies without telling
her of it. But this is not all of "Lukas Hoch-
strassers Haus" (Lukas Hochstrasser's House);
it is the tragedy of the father who is superior
to all his children, and dies without a successor.
"Die Frauen von Tanno" (The Women of
Tanno) is the story of a rare human conflict.
In a remote village a terrible malady persists
generation after generation, transmitted through
the mother. The women of Tanno belonging
to the families where the taint inheres are joined
into a league of maidenhood in order that the
disease may be stamped out. The story of these
nuns who walk in the world but yet, by one vow,
are not of the world, is one of tragic pathos.
The wife of "Stephan der Schmied" (Stephen
the Smith) dies in giving birth to a child which
is not his. The smith is of giant strength, violent in passion, but at heart an overgrown child.
Deaf to all remonstrances, he insists on naming
the child Cain; and upon the name itself hangs
much of the tale. Gradually the sullen severity
of the man yields to the child who bears the face
of the woman he had loved. Stephan is enraged
because the school-boys twit Cain with his name;
he moves away to be rid of the situation and
renames the youth Franz, but there is no real

escape; he has punished the innocent boy and clouded his own life. "Der Apotheker von Klein-Weltwyl" is an attempt to show the life of a whole community in relationship to a single motive for conduct, envy. The apothecary is a mysterious and partly symbolic character, somewhat Mephistophelean in his get-up. With uncanny omniscience he reveals to other people the bases of their actions.

Zahn's descriptions of Alpine scenery are constant, varied, and impressive. They are simple and direct, without rhetorical embellishment save for an occasional telling simile. The grandeur of their world is to the Swiss a pervasive presence, but they are not blinded to it by constant familiarity. So in these stories the landscape does not stand there for its own sake; it becomes a part of the narrative, because it is essentially a part of the lives recorded. Verena Stadler looks out over the lake at St. Felix. "The lake lay in dark leaden hue at her right. Far beyond stretched two dull surfaces, the sky and the motionless lake. But in the far distance, as if cut with a shining, keen-edged blade, a strange, gleaming, golden streak lay between sky and lake. There a sunbeam had broken its way through the mist. It was as if a curtain had been drawn back from another world, a sunny world of almost supernatural beauty; one could see into gleaming depths and distances. In them stood the vague outlines of the mountains, mysterious, as if just moved into the light. A beautiful field of pure snow lay close beneath the sky. The white surface shone like a holy altar, candle-lighted, in the choir of a dim church." Into Verena's mind there flashes a memory of lake and mountains on that day of happiness long ago. "Come," she says to the boy, the other woman's boy, and, taking him firmly by the hand, "she went resolutely, bravely, as it were, past her own youth."

So Stina Lussmann in "Das Muttergöttesli" (The Little Virgin), whose home had been made a place of infernal torment, stands and looks at her world. "Four mighty walls hem it in; here the black wood climbs up the walls, and there the snow-pale slopes draw close to them, and spread out between the forests, looking like corpse-faces with dark beards. Up there the steep gray walls project, their breasts clad in ice as with a coat of mail. The thick white mist which before has filled the whole valley, lies still over the bed of the brook. And down over this mist which extends like a column of smoke mountain-wards, on up to the village of Ober-Ebmeten, over the thick, strange web, the white, gleaming, holy, head of the Ewigschneehorn looks down. . . . In the sky there are red streaks in the cold blue; a glow, scarcely perceptible, burns about the white mountain. It seems to Stina as if it must be warm there." Though reason whispers, "down in the valley there is work," Stina cannot do otherwise, she begins to run slowly, and runs on and on, up toward the Ewigschneehorn. Liberius, the parish clerk, lonely in his joyless home, sits staring into vacancy, his head resting

in his hand. But suddenly he sees the sun lying
in the window. "The evening glow played between the leaves and flowers, here and there
deepening a colour wonderfully, or surrounding
a flower with a soft halo. It played too about
the gray-painted window frame. There was
something mysterious about it, as if some friendly
power had lighted for Liberius Arnold a little
candle outside the darkening room. He stood up
to see whence the warm golden light came, and
saw the sun standing in the West already close
to the line of the mountain tops. Now it touched
one of the mountains, and a shining and sparkling
was for a moment on the summit, as if the hard
stone had lured sparks from the impinging star
of light. Then the sun sank rapidly. The sheen
by the window and among the flowers grew pale."
Liberius's irritation is gone, and a pensive mood
possesses him.

But the glory and majesty of Swiss scenery are
but the remoter background for Zahn's stories.
In the foreground the little brown houses cluster,
climbing up the slopes, or lining the wind-free
valleys; high up like swallows' nests crouch the
cottages of those whose courage builds habitations close to the edge of timeless snows. "Along
the meadow way stood big brown farmsteads,
eight or so of them, looking down over the hill
into the plain and on the ampitheatre of mighty
mountains standing behind. Like velvet shone
the healthy, weather-browned wood of their
outer walls. A white or coloured curtain at this
window or that, a few yellow ears of maize hang-

ing to the eaves or a few carnation plants which let their flowers wave in the wind, added a touch of colour to the dark of the wood."

It will, perhaps, have been inferred that Zahn is not a teller of cheerful tales. He has little humour and no sense for the comic. Whether intended for tragedy or comedy, the story of the poor man with a large family who swallows a gold nugget, the inheritance from his brother, it is successful neither as one nor the other. Once or twice he seems wilfully to have preferred what is known as a "sad ending," as in "Kämpfe" (Conflicts), where the heroine drowns herself only a few hours before all had been well. In "Grundwasser" (The Depths Below) the power of blood and training yields for a time to a great resolve, but asserts itself once more, when through a chance misunderstanding the resolve is weakened, and later the most pitiful of all tragedies is enacted, the failure of heroic effort to rise above our dust. But generally the novelist provides for an ineradicable tragic principle which, quite independent of fortuitous circumstance, leads to unhappiness and failure. The words of Goethe's harper, "Every sin is punish'd here below" might be set as a motto for much of Zahn's work. Unerringly, according to his philosophy, a moral delinquency brings its punishment with it; but it is not for him to decide whether or not the punishment is commensurate with the offence. He has no inexorable system of measured retribution. Still less does he introduce familiar conceptions of guilt and reward.

The church plays, indeed, a conspicuous part in the lives of his characters; the mountain parsonage is the home of a Christ-like unselfishness, and the source of cheer and unfailing counsel, but life is never interpreted from a theological standpoint.

In one story after another the past rises like a malevolent ghost, and, whether or not the sun actually brings all secrets to the light of day, the agony of self-accusation and remorse is made the more potent because the deed and the emotional causation which stood behind it are now so far away and so loathed. The mental and emotional habits of these Swiss mountain folk make concealment of the past a natural course which needs no defence or explanation, but with the delayed disclosure there falls an accumulated weight of chastisement. Each lives so much of his life as a stranger to others; silent, uncommunicative, they walk beside one another; the garrulous peasants of sunnier lands tell all and more than all, but these mountaineers live the inward life with sealed lips, whether concealing good or ill.

"Das Leben der Salome Zeller" (The Life of Salome Zellar) is one long effort to hide a sin; constant necessity of lying worms into her nature, preys upon her, her whole life becomes a lie. After twenty years, that which no one would have deemed possible comes to light. A transgression hidden for many years and never disclosed is that of Violanta, the heroine of "Schatten" (Shadows). Yet the penalty is not wanting.

Reared in poverty and moral degradation, Violanta keeps herself from stain, save once when she listens to the moon-lit wiles of the gay lieutenant, Martinus Renner. Then Violanta goes out to service; splendid in her beauty and strength, capable and faithful, she earns a place of confidence among those whom she serves. Her employment brings her to the little upland village where lies the great farmstead home of the Renners. Martin's mother is a gentlewoman of dignity and force, and Adelreich, his brother, enjoys the esteem of the community for his integrity and for his efficient management of the estate. No one knows of Martin's whereabouts. The past trembles on Violanta's lips when Adelreich seeks her hand; he knows well the home from which she came and its reputation, but he sees only her present greatness. Years pass; Violanta as mistress of the household is loved and revered by all. Then Martin comes back, a wretched, inebriate tramp. He perceives his advantage and by a process of black-mail subjects Violanta to the rack of constant martyrdom. Finally she takes his life and then her own,— for the sake of her husband and her children. But no one ever suspects how it happened. In "Lentin" a dying father confesses to his boy a wrong which years before he had inflicted on a neighbour. Lentin takes up the burden of recompense; he serves a prison sentence of wretchedness in this very household, buffeted, abused, tormented, until he has paid the uttermost farthing of his father's guilt.

One of Zahn's collections of short stories is entitled "Was das Leben zerbricht" (What Life Shatters), and another "Helden des Alltags" (Everyday Heroes) ; and these two titles might be applied conjointly to all of his work in fiction. His stories tell of dreams shattered, of ambitions thwarted, of effort unrewarded. Life deals harshly with his world, cruelly indeed with love and fortune. Zahn is peculiarly convincing in portraying those times of life when the well-springs dry up and the enthusiasms burn low, when the fine impulse to "get ahead" yields to the willingness to "get along." The inspiration to assault and conquer deadens into a grumbling or placid resignation. But Zahn is not a pessimist, nor a fatalist. Though life seems ruthless and malevolent, he is not querulously resentful, but calmly seeks points of reconciliation;—a chief characteristic of Zahn's stories is their dignity and repose. His main purpose is to discover moral greatness in humble deeds and in misdirected effort, and he consoles us with his discoveries. Not that he tries to be an appraiser of moral values; he appears simply as an appreciator of them. His heroism is a moral heroism and is entirely removed from questions of success and failure. The task of living is a bitterly earnest and solemn thing; the physical temptations and restrictions, the iron grip of time, the irreconcilable wills of men, or the impenetrable barriers between man and man, lead in nearly all cases to disappointment and sorrow, but the moral heroism of the individual is something entirely apart; it stands like a Swiss mountain peak in the midst of storms, unapproachable, concealed at times, but unassailed and unchanged. This is Zahn's conclusion. The intensity of his insight and the verity of his accumulated evidence almost coerce us into an acquiescence in his views.

THE NOVEL OF THE GREAT WAR

IN discussing contemporary affairs it is far easier to be diverting than to be comprehensive or penetrating. This circumstance lends support to the familiar saying that criticism of current literature is merely "conversation." Any attempt at critical evaluation of current work becomes peculiarly presuming when conditions in the world at large tend to produce a torrent of partisanship which engulfs author, reader, and critic. The possible few who stand aside are incapable of valid judgments; an aloofness which would permit the requisite perspective would at the same time betoken an almost incredible incapacity for sympathy or an absorption in other interests which would be equally disqualifying.

The German novel of the war period arose at a time when it is hardly an exaggeration to say that there were no unbiassed persons in the belligerent lands, and few indeed, perhaps none, anywhere else. The whole world was caught up by a flaming flood, which in subsiding, has left most people in a kind of bewilderment on its parched banks, looking at the receding surge. For most of the world it is difficult to look up from one's own absorbing or even desperate concerns and face realities objectively. Yet German fiction of war days and post-war days challenges attention on several points. Out of the multitude which no man can number, a few novels possess, it may be, those qualities of life which make for enduring importance. Others,—and this would seem to supply at any rate a temporary significance,—disclose clearly and convincingly what the Germans were thinking about in those years when the thunder of artillery drowned all human voices. Fiction of this period affords an important basis for the study of national psychology, providing illustrations, inadequate and subsidiary perhaps but not negligible, of mass-opinion and mass-action.

Doubtless a considerable proportion of German fiction since 1914 has only the value of old newspaper files; it is a mine for the historian of the future. The stories present with considerable fulness the events of the war years, as they were chronicled in the public press; directly or indirectly they sought to interpret, instruct and exhort; they followed the war in all its phases, incorporating adventures on all fronts and experiences in every sort of service. The substance of these novels became, unquestionably, merged with the general impression of the war gained in other ways, the imagined events being inextricably mingled with the authentic. Incidentally it may be remarked that the non-German reader would do well to leave the German war novel alone, if he feels his gorge rise at German exultation over German victories,—unless to be sure he enjoys the experience.

To characterize the typical German war novel unreservedly as a product of commercialized patriotism would surely be unfair, but scores of authors are always ready to turn a penny, perhaps are under the financial necessity of doing so, and nothing is surer of a commercial success than that which seems to confirm what everyone believes already and wishes to believe. But all novelists were not content with the glittering surface of things. Some of them realized that the circumstances of the great war and its bearing on human destiny were by no means as simple as it suited the purpose of every nation to present them; it was not a nursery fable with a clear sundering of good and evil. To them, these hesitating, reluctant ones, there was something behind and beyond the annihilation of a hostile battery or a successfully devastating air raid. And some novelists, it would seem, did not trust themselves to speak of the war at all.

For German fiction, as for German military and political circumstance, the armistice inevitably stands as a milestone. Novels of war days, of battle-field and heroic effort, can never be quite the same as in the first years; the child-like singleness of outlook is now inconceivable; knowledge of the outcome darkens martial enthusiasms, even in retrospect, and the relationships between past and present are so intricate and variegated, seem so illogical and incredible that the novelist to-day is staggered at the thought of interpretation. The German people has travelled far since the earliest novels of the war. To the German who has merely accepted the new order as well as to him who is giving his devotion to stabilizing it, these novels appear like "documents out of long past time, when the

fairy-tale of a peace-loving people attacked by
spiteful neighbours . . . . still stood in its
spring-time bloom." He rubs his eyes in wonder
that he ever found pleasure or satisfaction in
them. Such tales were once useful fuel for the
furnace of patriotic passion, but there is now no
substance in their ashes, except, the cynic may
remark, for use with sack cloth.

The novels of Nanny Lambrecht, "Die eiserne
Freude" (Iron Joy) and "Die Fahne der Wal-
lonen" (The Banner of the Walloons), once
widely popular, are good specimens of these
early war stories, the former beginning to appear in a Berlin periodical as early as November,
1914. The two novels are connected through
the identity of some of the chief characters. As
in most novels of the Franco-Prussian War, or
of the Civil War in the United States, the convenient formula in both stories is the love of an
invading warrior for a maiden of the conquered
country. The theme is so trite and obvious that
one may be pardoned a touch of cynicism in observing the inescapability of its use. In "Die
eiserne Freude" a young German physician is
betrothed to a Belgian girl, indeed the outbreak
of the war interrupts the festivities attending the
betrothal. Later he accompanies the invading
host, and with an inevitability characteristic of
manufactured fiction, the fortunes of war bring
him to grips with those who were once his friends.
The brother of his former fiancée is shot as a
franc-tireur, and her father is imprisoned, yet
the girl herself seeks her lover and openly es-

pouses his cause. The story is interwoven with revolting acts on the part of the Belgian population, the kind of report current in Germany during the first months of the war, and here related with considerable gusto. The invaders themselves are portrayed as valiant, knightly warriors, long-suffering toward an irritating, untrustworthy people, but eventually unrelenting as instruments of a justified wrath. The second novel assumes a somewhat more conciliatory attitude toward the Belgians, in presenting them as childish dupes of the allied powers, chiefly England; gallant Belgians, awakened from their deception, go to their death resisting the arrogant ally. The stories are narrated with passable skill, are smooth and simple in style, and capable in execution; they are filled with stirring adventures, almost every page being supplied with its thrill—spies, disguises, hiding-places, acts of superhuman audacity, of physical prowess and reckless bravery. Their popularity is understandable.

An interesting contrast between the earlier war novel and the novel of post-war days is afforded by the two most recent stories of Gustav Frenssen, "Die Brüder" (The Brothers) and "Der Pastor von Poggsee." One was written at the flood tide of enthusiasm and even boisterous confidence, and the second novel in the desolation of bewildered defeat. They are interesting documents.

In choice of scene and characters, Frenssen knows and loves his own; he is not easily de-

flected into fresh fields. The central scene of
"Die Brüder," to which the events of the plot,
after brief absences, are ever returning, is a
farmstead in Holstein, the home of the Ott
family. Though Frenssen endeavours to dif-
ferentiate the members of this family, is obviously intent on relating their several qualities
to their environment, to the impact of personalities on one another in a narrow community,
"Mother" Ott is the only one who stands out
as a memorable figure. Strength without arrogance, solidity without heaviness, simplicity
and utter guilelessness, are her characteristics;
her ends she accomplishes through singleness of
purpose and through the exercise of qualities
which in different social circles one would call
dignity and tact. She rules her home with reason-
able orderliness, and always sacrifices herself
rather than demand a sacrifice of others. There
is a distinct suggestion that Frenssen has consciously drawn her as his ideal of German womanhood, his "Frau Germania."

To set his plot in motion, Frenssen makes use
of a trivial incident. A mysterious whistle is
heard several times about the place, the source
of which is disclosed years afterwards. The
stable-boy is the culprit, having learned a ventril-
oquist's trick from a band of strolling players.
This uncanny occurrence sets the whole family
by the ears; Emma, the daughter, flushed with
religious fervour in the adolescent period, is
seriously unstrung and takes to her bed; Father
Ott attributes the disturbing sounds to Eggert, the

fourth son, who resents the charge, quarrels
with his father, and leaves home, vowing that
he will never return. His former sweetheart
betrays the fact that he has sought a refuge in
America, and later, Harm, his older brother,
now employed on a German steamship, seeks him
there. This circumstance leads Frenssen to include a brief description of New York which,
though curious, is not as fantastic as the ac-
counts given by some German novelists who had
actually been there,—H. H. Ewers, for example,
in his recent war novel "Vampyr." Eggert has
already left New York, but Harm finds his
former landlady in the Bronx. That neither
this landlady nor her husband is willing to accept money from Harm for board, a brother
thus faithfully seeking the lost, is noted as a
proof that they have not as yet become real
Americans. But before Harm succeeds in carrying his quest further, rising war clouds send
his ship scurrying back to German waters. From
this point on, Frenssen's story becomes a war
novel.

Harm, entering the navy, is stationed on a
converted merchant ship patrolling the North
Sea. In a scene of melodramatic effectiveness,
he finds his brother Eggert on a Norwegian ves-
sel, bound from Boston to Rotterdam; the ship
has already been taken by the English, and an
English prize crew is on board, which, however,
is hidden on the approach of the German patrol.
Eggert had insisted on disclosing to the Germans
the presence of the concealed English crew, and

was then imprisoned with them. That Harm discovers his brother is, according to the laws of fiction, quite unavoidable. Later Harm is transferred to the cruiser "Below" and takes part in the battle of Skaggerak. This supplies Frenssen with an opportunity for a vivid description of a great sea fight, which is presumably intended as a companion piece to his now famous account of the Battle of Gravelotte in "Jörn Uhl." The alleged German victory over the Mistress of the Seas is selected by the novelist as a triumphant note for the close of his book. Eggert, entering the service, is wounded, and Reimer, another brother, is killed. The latter's eagerness to serve is doubtless intended to represent the common devotion of all, even of those who were physically inferior and inclined to bookish ways. The eldest brother, Klaus, who is married when the story opens, runs away from the post where his company is stationed, and hides himself at home. At this juncture, his mother interposes, and leads him, walking with him the whole night through, back to his forsaken duty. These are "The Brothers."

Frenssen's story contains episodes of arresting and at times thrilling power, but, as a whole, it loses much through a scattering of interest. A novel does not require a hero, but there must be some focus of attention, and Frenssen does not succeed, if that is his intent, in securing this position either for the Ott family or for the fortunes of Germany in the prodigious struggle. The outbreak of the war splits the novel in two, and the first part seems like the beginning of another story, for the novelist, when the time comes, fails to make the Ott family carry the burden of his message; indeed, he bears this burden largely himself. For this reason the novel suffers from the obtrusiveness of his purpose; it does not bear the weight easily. It is not at all that he reiterates in Germany's defense a now thrice-told tale, — the unparalleled devotion of a whole people, the innocence of evil intent, the unprovoked attack of "robber" nations, the comradeship in army and navy, and the absence of all class distinctions in the presence of the common need; these matters Frenssen loads upon the story, rather than allows the story to unfold them. To-day too, the end of the novel in exultant joy over the Battle of Skaggerak seems no longer an effective terminus. That it appears now curiously inept in its premature conclusiveness is an accident of history.

In "Die Brüder" an ageing patriot contributed what one was wont to call "his bit" to the common cause. But a new, a far deeper concern for the fortunes of his fatherland possesses him when the fires of a hasty but natural enthusiasm have burned down. The German people sits down at its meagre board, in its shadowed rooms, and communes with its memories. As reflection is a richer experience than physical activity, as doubt is more interesting than assurance, Frenssen's later novel "Der Pastor von Poggsee" is incomparably more significant, more moving than the novel of 1917.

Adam Barfood, the hero of the new novel is
one of Frenssen's most sturdy creations, and
Frenssen traces his career with evident relish.
He is the son of a poor carpenter in a lonely
Holstein village. Faithfulness to obligations,
and cheerfulness, unfailing in quantity but somewhat syrupy in quality, do not prevent want and
distress from occupying the cottage with the
family, and difficulties are intensified when the
carpenter dies. Yet, somehow or other, the
widow contrives to get on; the girls are soon
old enough to go out into service, and Adam,
who attracts the attention of his teachers, apparently because he is merely less dull than
the other boys, is selected for encouragement
and is assisted through school and university,
eventually to the position of country parson.
But Adam is really a peasant, from the beginning
showing more taste for farm labour than for
theological subtleties, and he remains a peasant
to the end of the chapter. Simplicity, directness,
frankness to the verge of brutality, mark his intercourse with his parishioners; he is a peasant
among peasants. And in his qualities as a peasant
pastor lies the chief fascination of his character.

Although his career as a theological student,
competing with others in intellectual processes,
was rather dubious, and his later theological
vagaries attracted the attention of his superiors,
the authorities, when once under the spell of his
personality, were quite disarmed; there lay a
spiritual force behind his stubborn ignorance and
his unblushing naïveté which they had sufficient

wisdom to let alone. Adam's first pastorate is
in the two Holstein fishing villages of Hopptrupp
and Holebüll, among a class of people almost
incredibly ignorant, superstitious, and brutal.
And here through his simplicity, his overbearing
mastery, coupled with a paternal tenderness,
Adam wins his way. He did not scorn to work
as his people worked. His big, solid frame, his
rude, uncouth hands, brought him closer to them;
and he met their superstitions with some more
wholesome superstitions of his own, which no
theological study was ever able to eradicate.
After several years Adam is transferred to Poggsee, decidedly a preferment, though Poggsee is
itself a rural community where ignorance is at
home and social amenities are rare.

And it is here that the war overtakes the story.
Fortune is especially cruel to the Pastor of
Poggsee, and he becomes a veritable modern
Job. His two sons are killed at the front, one
of his daughters, married to the son of a neighbouring parson, dies as an indirect victim of war-
time woe; his house is burned over his head, and
the work of years in paying his own debts and
in aiding his family is set at naught; his enemies
even contrive to besmirch his name, and impugn
his integrity. But Adam, like his prototype,
never wavers. His faith in the divinity of humanity is unshaken; unwearied and selfless are
his ministrations; he does not flinch even when
the sufferers are those who have spitefully mis-
used and persecuted him. The blunt, crude,
peasant clergyman takes on heroic lines. His

looseness of theological thinking is doubtless Frenssen's own, as has been amply attested by earlier stories. Yet it may be questioned whether or not one is justified in attributing to Frenssen himself his pastor's seemingly limitless extension of Christ's compassion for the woman taken in sin; it is carried to the point where there would seem to be no inviolable bases left for the regulation of human relationships; his championship of every woman's right to motherhood is tinged with vapid sentiment.

Frenssen's interpretation of the war, whether he uses Adam or others as his spokesman, yields no absolutely clear outline. It is often plainly the work of a man whose intellect and emotions are in conflict. Thus in many of his longer discourses, particularly in the long speech which Adam delivers at a great folk festival, when the war is over, he falls into the pit which always yawns for him who can not maintain his emotional equilibrium; like many an orator, he starts out with the resolve to be impartial; "come now let us reason together," he seems to say, but as he speaks and perforce must touch matters which act as emotional stimuli, he forgets his principles, and froths in insensate rage.

According to Frenssen's account, there was at the beginning of the war no shout of enthusiasm in German villages, no joy in the war;—rather a nameless, abysmal sadness that the destiny of mankind had fallen into the hands of murderers and incendiaries,—a dumb despair because one's faith in mankind was broken. An unshakable conviction that the fatherland, both rulers and people, had not desired the war, had consciously done nothing to provoke it, made such an accusation on the part of the outside world a sword that entered every heart. And yet there is full acknowledgment of errors which alienated Germany from the sympathy of her neighbours. To Bismarck's ruthless disregard of others' rights the German people were blind, simply because they were grateful to him for the unification of Germany and for the prosperity which followed it. Germans were arrogant and boastful, indiscreet and loud-mouthed in their relationships with other peoples. And prosperity brought an unutterable avarice in its train; "that the whole world turned against us we did not see; we were blinded by the gleam of gold." The lack of unity among the German people, the cleft between the upper and lower classes, the one with a monarchical, the other with a democratic ideal, is held responsible in large part for Germany's downfall. Further, the Germans did not have the moral strength and depth to withstand the deleterious effects of prosperity; "fire we had, but it turned to ashes." The war is God's judgment, the rod of His chastisement, which at the same time points back to the forsaken pathway of righteousness. From this idea, through the lips of his pastor, Frenssen builds up his hopes for the future, and in a last impassioned passage, he advances the conviction that the real victory belongs to those who have suffered inconceivably and thereby have grown strong and pure.

Frenssen's stories are all defective in construction; the plot is either conventional with melodramatic embroideries, or is simply curious and unconvincing. Here, as in "Die Brüder," the elements which the novelist invents to supply tension and thereby to excite interest are inept and unimpressive. The villain, Holgersen, who first makes his appearance at Holebüll as a mysterious, seductive personality, and reappears at Poggsee as the church sexton, is a stagy figure; and his malign influence at Poggsee, his extensive and eccentric thievery, primarily of precious church vessels, and his final leadership of disordered elements in rebellion against the new republic, seem awkwardly and dubiously contrived; they do not move us mightily, we seem to perceive too clearly their function in creating obstacles for Adam to overcome. As in "Die Brüder," the novel is cut in twain by the outbreak of the war, but the character of the pastor is strong enough to keep the structure from falling asunder. He possesses a kind of rude grandeur like an unfinished statue in the sculptor's workshop. One point more should not pass unnoted. The latter part of Frenssen's story contains heart-rending and vivid descriptions of miseries endured during the last years of the war, the all-prevailing hunger, the crowds of mothers with starving children who fled from the cities and thronged the country roads, begging for food, the breaking down of law and of respect for law, the loosening of every moral inhibition, the gaunt and horrid omnipresence of crime.

228 The Modern German Novel

A very similar impression is made by Otto
Ernst's popular novel "Hermannsland" (Hermann's Land); that is, in the relation of imagined circumstance, the bitterness of a resentment which had perhaps been put away, is suddenly revivified, and the war is fought over again.
Thirty years ago Otto Ernst put the world in his
debt by publishing one of the most charming
stories of childhood which literature has to show,
"Asmus Sempers Jugendland" (Asmus Semper:
The Land of his Boyhood), though indeed Asmus
becomes less interesting as he grows older in
"Semper der Jüngling" (Semper the Youth)
and "Semper der Mann" (Semper the Man).
With allowances for difference of place and race,
particularly for over-abundant sentiment,—
nevertheless characteristic and hence pertinent,—
one might compare "Asmus Sempers Jugendland"
with Hugh Walpole's "Jeremy," or Kenneth
Graham's "Golden Age."

And "Hermannsland" begins with an enticing
promise of similar pleasure. The first two-
thirds of the book present the boyhood and youth
of the hero, Hermann Stahmer, his school-days,
and his friendships. Though Hermann's parents
are decidedly well-to-do, his bosom friend, Gracchus Ohlenfleth, is a boy from the labouring
classes. One may revel in the adventures of
these two boys, in the variegated world about
them, made more complicated by the difference
in their social station, and later, in the golden
world of books which they discover together.
But boyhood gives way to young manhood, to

university years. Then the war casts its shadows
over their work and play. Gracchus had absorbed
the socialistic notions of his class; his first and
only quarrel with Hermann was about Bismarck
and the system for which Bismarck stood; in attending the university, he accepts at first financial
aid from Hermann's father, but later he declines
to be dependent on one whose social and political
thinking differ so radically from his own. But
with the outbreak of the war, all his theories are
forgotten. The last third of the story relates
the war-time experiences of the two friends.
Hermann is wounded, and Gracchus is captured
and held a prisoner in France. According to
Otto Ernst, every fiendish outrage was per-
petrated by the French, soldiers and civilians
alike, on captive Germans, especially on German officers, of whom the French were actually
afraid, even though they were prisoners. It is
in narrating such matters as these that the novelist loses his balance and falls back into the confused violence of other years. He shouts to the
world his vituperative hatred of the foe, which
like a pack of angry wolves had wantonly attacked the noblest of all nations. England is
called the "unspeakable prostitute," who set
about to poison the world. The down-fall of
Germany is attributed in considerable part to
this basest of English villainies. A story which
begins with sweet reasonableness, with dignity
and beauty, is turned into a fish-wife's tirade; the
novelist's passion becomes farcical rather than
impressive.

A considerable number of historical novels published in war days or soon after may be regarded as war novels, since they bear a recognizable even though indirect relationship to the war itself. Through an enlivening of the German past, particularly of times when the situation seems parallel to the circumstances of the present, these novels sought to inculcate patriotism and to foster the whole array of personal and national virtues most needed at such times. Georg von Ompteda, who had not written a novel for a number of years broke his silence with a novel called "Es ist Zeit" (The Time Has Come), a vivid, though overwrought and subjective tale of the Tyrolese insurrection in 1809. The sacrificial devotion of Andreas Hofer and his comrades is related anew, but gains little through the telling. Ompteda's emotions run riot with his judgment, and his style becomes wearisome in its high-sounding dithyrambs.

To the same class belong Walter von Molo's historical stories. A couple of years before the beginning of the war Molo published the first of his cycle of four novels on the life of Schiller, a series which was completed in the early years of the conflict, and in itself was not ill calculated to stir a reminiscent patriotism. In the heart of the world war Molo encouraged himself and others through studies of the Prussian royal house, finding stimulating themes, so he thought, in the lives of Frederick the Great and Queen Louise. The appeal of such books, whether the subject be a beloved poet or an honoured monarch, is usually to undiscerning minds; nursery intelligences are pleasantly intrigued by a work of fiction which seems to bring a revered personality into closer view. The unfailing method is to supply a mass of everyday domestic detail, a king laying aside his crown and playing leap-frog with his boys, or a queen soothing the tooth-ache of a princess. These Hohenzollern novels served as parables of patriotism, and the critical approval which they have enjoyed can hardly be called unbiassed; at the time it was doubtless especially difficult to be objective. Naturally to a non-German reader their patriotic fervour is neither a merit, nor necessarily a fault; their value must be judged on other grounds. Molo has visualized his historical periods with real skill and power, he has his eye also on the deeper meaning of events, has essayed a real interpretation of the past. And he has instilled into his stories a considerable measure of poetic beauty. These qualities may preserve his historical novels from being eventually packed away with the imaginary disclosures of the industrious Miss Mühlbach.

Max Dreyer's "Nachwuchs" (Descendants), a story of the Napoleonic wars, and of the years immediately following them, is still another novel in which the events of other times are used with the tacit confidence that the reader will make an application to the present. "Nachwuchs" is written around a prayer said to have been spoken by a German pastor in those days when the wars of Napoleon had decimated the manhood of Europe: "Lord, bless the wombs of our wives,

that they bring forth men-children, for the sword
has consumed the men of the land, and it is of
men that the fatherland stands in need." In
Dreyer's novel a childless wife voluntarily be-
stows her husband upon another, a widow of
the war, that sons may be raised up for the
fatherland; in another instance, the case of a
subordinate character, illegitimacy is, by implication, condoned; for men are needed. Another
historical novel by Max Dreyer, "Der deutsche
Morgen" (The German Dawn) seeks to derive
wisdom and consolation from the past. It begins
with the return of warriors from the Napoleonic
conflict, but is concerned primarily with questions
of freedom and patriotism, of suppression and
persecution in the period following the Congress
of Vienna. The hero is a professor in Berlin
whose utterances disturb the vigilant police officials; he is arrested and tried; his friends arrange to rescue him as he is being taken to the
fortress where he is to be incarcerated; but he
himself is mortally wounded in the struggle which
ensues. The story ends theatrically and il-
logically with the arrival of Bismarck in Berlin
as a school-boy. This event is utterly uncon-
nected with the narrative as a whole, but it serves
as a kind of prophecy that the dreams which the
chief characters of the story have cherished are
eventually to be realized, that the longed-for
dawn is yet coming.

It would be natural that discussion in regard
to Alsace-Lorraine would be revived. Had
slumbering fires, carefully covered, gone out in

the half-century since 1870? The problems of
the disputed territory have frequently been the
theme of French as well as of German fiction,
for example in the work of Maurice Barrès and
René Bazin. The war bestowed a new pertinence
on the question. The content of stories about
Alsace is usually easily inferred from the situation; it is a question of loyalties, one political
allegiance, one cultural allegiance, has officially
been supplanted by another. The erasure of the
old loyalties is a process which moves forward
with different speed in different people, and the
misunderstandings which arise during the substitution supply the material for this kind of novel.
Naturally acute crises are produced when circumstances test loyalty or array one set of loyalties against another set.

Anselma Heine, for example, with her eye on
the war in progress tells a story of 1870 and
subsequent years, to which she gives the significant title "Die verborgene Schrift" (The Hidden Writing). According to her interpretation,
the lost provinces, now in the Franco-Prussian
War regained, have never at bottom ceased to
be German; they were like a mediæval pal-
impsest; beneath the modern handwriting, there
lies, at times obscured but still permanent and
indelible, the original German text, inalienable
German culture. Much more important is Fritz
Lienhard's recent story "Westmark" (The
Western Borderland), written after the fortunes
of war had returned the provinces to France.
Lienhard, himself an Alsatian, is not a stranger

to the affairs of Alsace, which form the most
conspicuous experiment of modern times in
attempted alteration of cultural allegiance; his
best known work is the long novel "Oberlin," a
story of Alsace in the epoch of the French Revolution, which figures as its most significant character,—though not as the hero of the plot,—the
historical Oberlin, a famous Protestant pastor of
those days. In "Westmark" Lienhard makes one
of the characters a descendant of Oberlin. There
is no chauvinism about Lienhard; he is inclined
to a reconciliatory view of things; and there is
but a trace of bitterness in the full chalice of his
grief. He thinks the war a universal error, a
world calamity, and bemoans the fatal treaty as
a stain on the fair fame of all who framed it.
The substance of the story is trite, and the plot
conventional. A division of sympathies arrays
neighbour against neighbour, a father against his
children, a lover against his loved one, and the
irreconcilables go into exile. By far the most
notable thing in Lienhard's book is the little
dedicatory poem in which the author voices his
high hopes for his prostrate fatherland. Lienhard derives comfort from the fact that Weimar
and the Wartburg remain, though the beloved
border provinces are gone, and then,—as it were,
holding in mind the Psalmist's words: "Except
the Lord keep the city, they labour in vain that
build it"—he goes on to say: "The empire without a soul broke in fragments; before the whole
world we stand in shame. Now it is our place
to build up out of light an empire of the soul

which can not be shattered. Here, German
youth, lies your pathway! Give New Germany
a soul!"

A peculiar interest attaches to a group of
novels which have been called pacifistic or defeatist. We might not like to be questioned as
to the sources of our satisfaction in them. One
is perhaps stirred to a retroactive triumph in
learning that there were Germans or Austrians
who raised Cassandra voices in the market-place
in the very flush of Teutonic success, and found
in material gains no real compensation for
spiritual losses. It would, however, be a sorry
experience if these books served only to nurture
our complacency. Their significance goes far
deeper than any superficial appeal to our war-
time prepossessions. The typical war novel is
checked by a narrowed vision; it represents, perhaps inevitably, the attitude of the man who says
to himself; "This one thing I do. I have neither
time nor inclination to question it, or to reflect
upon it." On the other hand, the merit of such
books as Barbusse's "Le Feu" or Dos Passos's
"Three Soldiers" does not lie in their telling us
things about the great war which we do not know,
nor in their persistent gloating over the hideous
aspects of it; indeed, the accumulation of these
things, through over-stress, tends to irritate us
and arouse distrust; but rather, by constant implication, they look beyond to-day; they pause
to ask about the warrior's larger self, his peace-
time self; they express a wholesome scepticism
for inconsiderate and manipulated enthusiasms;

they communicate a sense of human dignity un-
speakably outraged. A novel written as a plea
against war is, of course, not necessarily superior
to the most blindly belligerent tale. But, at any
rate for the time being, the defeatist or pacifistic
book is likely to make its appeal to the intellectual, the reflective side of man's nature; it tries
to estimate more than one kind of values.

So the two war novels of Clara Viebig pierce
us to the quick, stir us, and overwhelm us, as
no swashbuckling romance, no dashing tale of
cavalry charges or air-plane exploits has as yet
been able to do. The two novels form practically one story, the second book, "Das rote
Meer" (The Red Sea) taking up the characters
of "Töchter der Hekuba" (Hecuba's Daughters)
where they were left and carrying them on to
the end of the war. "Das rote Meer" is appreciably weaker in substance and form, partially
from mere repetition of material, and partly because of a diminished spontaneity in handling it.
The scene of both stories is a suburban region
near Berlin where a congeries of smart new villas
together with their inhabitants has been super-
imposed upon a community still essentially rural.
Thus a considerable diversity of character and
interest is obtained, a chance propinquity serving
to bind characters together for the purposes of
the novelist. The great war involves the lives
of all, one after another, in a net-work of tragic
circumstance, but the novelist has not tried to
construct a real plot.

As the title, "Daughters of Hecuba," suggests, the narrative is concerned with the wives and daughters of warriors. Clara Viebig never visits the battle-front; there are no scenes of armed encounter, no thrill of military glory, drum-beat, or bugle-call. For the most part these lives are led hundreds of miles from any kind of military peril; the visible surface of things is unchanged; the tasks of life remain the same, though different people in part are doing them. Yet the art of the novelist contrives to make it all more tragic than a battle-field, more starkly awful than burning villages and unknown graves. Life which has been full and free becomes a dull, monotonous, featureless waste. One goes through prescribed forms for the mere maintenance of physical living; but these women, time dragging like heavy chains upon their weariness, become gradually conscious that their world at the front and at home is not really fighting for anything any more, at any rate not for anything recogniz-able or desirable. In the midst of familiar scenes, it is as if some evil spirit had seized the substance of everyday living and twisted it be-yond recognition.

Early in her career as a story-teller, Clara Viebig wrote a short novel called "Das Weiber-dorf" (The Village of Women), in which she portrays with considerable humour the situation in a remote German village where ordinarily for the better part of the year all or nearly all of the men are away at work. In certain aspects this earlier story may be considered as a pre-

liminary study for the war novels. The circumstances are in part repeated; in the war
novels, the women are left behind with the old
men, as time goes by, only with the very old
men, and the children,—and gradually too, with
a pitiful host of broken, scarred, unrecognizable
beings which once were men. The village becomes a feminine community, every kind of
labour, public and private, is performed by
women. As may be readily inferred, in the later
novel as in the former, Clara Viebig does not
fail to admit the erotic elements which in the
given circumstances are likely to appear; but in
1916 there is no place for even a semi-humorous
display of them.

Frau Krüger, pitifully poor in her little house
and garden, has heard no news from her son
Gustav for many months. In an illustrated
paper she finds a picture of German prisoners
held at Malta, and she clings passionately to the
conviction that she recognizes Gustav among
them; she can not be shaken in her belief; "I am
his mother, don't I know him?" she exclaims.
Gustav had loved a working-girl, Gertrud Hiesel-
hahn, of whom his mother had disapproved, and
when he is at home on a furlough, she prevents
his marrying her by insinuating that he is perhaps
not the only one to whom one might ascribe the
paternity of the child which has been born.
Gertrud is dignified and self-respecting; she
works to support herself and her child,—endless
hours of toil,—and does not murmur. As time
goes by, Frau Krüger becomes more and more

lonely; she has only a picture to cherish, and in
Gertrud's little boy whom she sees by chance,
she recognizes the features of her missing son.
She accepts Gertrud as her daughter and takes
her to her home.   Later Gertrud marries a
soldier who has been wounded beyond patching
up for further service; he has been a comrade of
Gustav's and, after his discharge, he seeks out
the widow Krüger to bring her news of Gustav's
death, and to deliver his last messages for those
he loved.   This incident brings to our attention
a new type of profiteer; there was, it appears,
in the latter part of the war a large amount of
swindling and chicanery in the appearance of
alleged comrades who fabricated death-scenes
and loving messages, naturally in return for food,
lodging, or money, from those to whom they
came.

Minna Dombrowski, in whose cottage Gertud
rents a room, is a weak, sensual woman, handsome in a brutish sort of way, fond of finery
which she can afford now even less than before
her husband went off to war.   Now the dull
routine of life, duller still through its depriva-
tions, irks her sorely; the care of her two children
wearies her, and she steals away to Berlin, and
human relationships become to her mainly, if not
entirely, animal.   So her husband, returning for
a brief furlough, discovers her in all her faith-
lessness, and departs never to return.   Minna
finds employment as a section hand on a railway
track; here she is killed by a passing train, as
she gazes abstractedly after another train which

bears one of her lovers back to the western front.

Higher social circles are represented by the families of General von Voigt and General Bertholdi. Lili, a daughter of General von Voigt, had married an Italian some years before the outbreak of the war. She wavers for a time in her allegiance, but becomes thoroughly German in sentiment, even before her gallant husband is killed on the Piave. Later she falls in love with Heinz Bertholdi, who is at home on a furlough. She is incomparably lovely in her youth, and fascinating in the elaborate mourning which she wears for the dead Italian, and Heinz becomes her prisoner, though as yet no word of love is spoken. At the end of the war Heinz comes back blind, and the devotion of the two to one another is a touch of wan autumn sunshine with which "Das rote Meer" ends. Lili is by nature shallow and selfish, but experience brings its floods to cover her incompetence, and her character is ennobled. Far different is the case of Annemarie, whom Rudolf Bertholdi marries at the beginning of the war. Her love of pleasure, her delight in millinery, meet hardly a momentary check in the news of Rudolf's death at the front. She has no organ for the understanding of deeper things; she chafes at the restraints which convention puts upon her; she wearies even of the picturesque aspects of her grief, and seeks an excuse to profit from "a change," visiting a German watering-place not far from the western front which is apparently one vast brothel. Frau

von Voigt and Frau Bertholdi take up the burdens
of their station in the community and assist in
the task of food regulation and distribution, in
soup-kitchens, and in other relief work. The
former illustrates the type of military aristocrat
whose prepossessions are inflexible. Her work
for the poor and wretched is unwearying, to be
sure, whether it is physical want or a burden of
sorrow which she is trying to assuage. In every
case, however, she is still the lady of the castle
distributing her largesse. In time those whom
she seeks to aid begin to jeer quite openly at her
confidence in the fatherland's solicitude for their
welfare, or at her insistence that distinctions of
class do not exist in military service; they find
the condescending aristocrat incredibly naïve.
There comes a time when the terms "militär-
fromm" and "königstreu" are used of her in
derision.

Frau Bertholdi works with tenderer touch.
She is equally tireless, but her heart is broader,
her understanding more complete. The sea of
horror and misfortune has undermined and en-
gulfed all she knows and loves; its surge and
flow obliterate gradually the prejudices of her
class; her motherliness is ready to care for the
outcast, to forgive and overlook offences, to see
in men and women merely suffering errant
children of a common Father.

And there are many others in these unforget-
able books, daughters of Hecuba, bearing their
woes, from the forsaken servant girls to the
mother who has lost her three sons, and spends

her days counting off on her fingers: "One, two, three! One, two, three!" And all the human woes are there, hunger of mother and child unsatisfied, the hideous cold and the awful dark; every form of grief is there too, born of diversity of loss and deprivation; and, above all, collectively, the collapse of moral standards, the withering of one's dreams, the haggard misery of the questioner who wonders what it was all about, the agony of those who curse God and still can not die.

Not more significant but more widely heralded are the pacifistic books of Andreas Latzko, an Austrian, "Menschen im Krieg" (Men in War), and "Friedensgericht" (The Judgment of Peace), and Leonhard Frank's "Der Mensch ist gut" (Man is good). Latzko's first book has been rather indifferently translated into English under the title "Men in War." It consists of a series of sketches, and is not really a novel. Like Barbusse, his French comrade of protest, Latzko seeks to overwhelm his readers with undreamed of horrors. Pages upon pages might flippantly be called "adventures with corpses," or more revoltingly still, "with pieces of corpses." The changes on this theme are rung, it would seem, through the whole gamut of military possibility. The book drips with blood, with brains, and entrails. Man made in the image of God is turned through man's greed, through an anachronism called war, into mere filth and stench. Latzko is a complete pacifist; he attacks all people who consent to war, individually and col-

lectively. For example, the women are as
culpable as the men; to Latzko the supposedly
inspiring spectacle of patriotism and self-sacrifice
attending the departure of troops is false and
despicable; the women who send their own away
with encouragement are sentimental cowards.
"Friedensgericht" is available in an admirable
English translation. In contrast with "Menschen
im Krieg" it has the merit of being one consecutive narrative, though its substance is hardly
more than a series of related incidents inter-
spersed with polemical discussion, albeit distinctly
pertinent and forceful. Its hero commits suicide
rather than return to active service.

The title of Leonhard Frank's book discloses
the angle from which he approaches his theme.
It resembles Latzko's first work in being a series
of episodes rather than a consecutive narrative,
but Frank has succeeded not only in binding the
episodes together extrinsically by their common
motive, but he provides as well a passable, if
somewhat fantastic, scheme for tying his incidents
into a constructive unit. In the first episode, the
hero is a waiter in a restaurant, capable, obliging,
and essentially high-minded. All his ambitions
centre in his boy for whom he secures every advantage which industry and loving self-sacrifice
can provide; he was not to be a waiter, through
a university education he was to attain a position
in another class. But the boy is killed in the
war, through his death seeming to take from his
father the only reason for existence. But one
day after weeks of brooding, he is serving drinks

to members of a patriotic club; he listens to its president mumbling the threadbare phrases of patriotic oratory, and remembers the little leaden soldiers of his dead boy, and the subsequent train of military festivals and fatherland enthusiasms which have led the way to an unknown grave somewhere in France. The iniquity and idiocy of it all rise and smite him with overwhelming force; he breaks into the patriotic ardour of the club meeting with his scathing denunciation and, napkin over his arm, this simple waiter leads unnumbered hosts, streaming from every street, in a procession of protest so tremendous that peace is won. Other episodes take up the grief of a wife whose husband has been killed, of a mother whose voice cries across the impassable barriers to other mothers in all lands, whose sons are lost to them, have been "crucified" for naught,—of a girl whose lover is dead. In the last chapter the novelist seemingly seeks to outdo all competitors in his descriptions of mutilated human beings; the scene is a make-shift operating-room where wounded soldiers are cut to pieces. Frank's narrative is overwhelming and he intends it to be. Like the great procession which the waiter leads and others have joined, the surgeon in charge of these human shambles heads a train of war cripples, men without arms, without legs, men bent double, men without faces, a man with neither arms nor legs, an army of inconceivable woe. All men are brothers, "man is good," we have only to remember the love which we have forgotten, and the devastating monster of the ages is tamed!

By birth and training Fritz von Unruh was of the caste which professionalized war and gloried in it, but during the war itself he turned from it with abhorrence and became in thought a German comrade of Romain Rolland. A volume of sketches called "Opfergang" (The Way of Sacrifice) is his contribution to war-time fiction. Within narrow limits, a couple of hundred pages, Unruh contrives to present a complete and over-whelming picture,—dug-outs, trenches, mire, ver-min, attacks and counter-attacks, disease and death, mutilation and corruption, and human beings, existing in this abyss of torment and exhibiting in various characteristic ways their nobler or their meaner selves. Unruh's realism, though unafraid, is somewhat more restrained, less patently straining for effect than the realism of many pacifistic stories, and perhaps on this very account his purposes are more unquestionably at-tained. Interwoven with the hideous reality of the present are dreams of home and thoughts of God; Unruh makes also at times a very effective use of symbol, for example—in a church which is used as a field hospital a demented soldier takes the crown of thorns from the head of a statue of Christ and calls it "barbed wire."

The pathetic stories of Herbert von Eulenberg to which he has given the significant title "Der Bankrott Europas" (Europe in Bankruptcy), may also be reckoned among the more important anti-war voices in German fiction. They are graceful in form, for the most part excellent examples of the short story which contains one salient point, works for effect and attains it by means of a single motive carefully worked out. Sometimes Eulenberg allows his imagination a freer rein, as in the little sketch "Zwei Pferde" in which he represents two horses, a German horse and a Russian horse, one of them dying, as discussing their masters and their masters' war. The motive is, of course, by no means new, but it is capable of very effective use, and Eulenberg has not failed of the satirical force which the situation allows.

The little story "Mutter," written by the woman who uses the pseudonym Hans von Kahlenberg is also a powerful anti-war document. "Mutter" purports to be the diary of a mother whose only son was killed in action near the beginning of the war; it is, however, hardly a diary in the sense of a consecutive record of events, but rather a series of meditations and reminiscences. From the sanctity of motherhood she derives her plea for the sanctity of the life it gives and her malediction upon war as contrary to every human interest and every divine principle.

By chance circumstance Heinrich Mann's novel "Der Untertan," which has been rendered into English under the title "The Patrioteer," appears to us in the guise of a war novel, or more exactly, of a novel prompted by reflection on the war and its causes. The book was really completed in July, 1914, but was not published

till the overthrow of the monarchy allowed
various forbidden things to walk in the light of
day. Our persistent impression of a post-war attitude in the novel itself, combined with our
knowledge of its actual date, lends a curious slant
to our enjoyment of the story. Mann has set
out to write a satire on "Kaiserism;" he invents
a hero, a veritable Hudibras of German militarism, and supplies a series of episodical adventures
to illustrate his imbecilities. That the theme in-
vited burlesque may be granted, but Mann is a
little heavy-handed, and the satire, particularly
in view of the attempt to sustain it, loses somewhat of its force.

To Diederich the obligation of "Kaisertreue"
is the motive force in living; he interrupts trivial
and important matters, casual or significant under-
takings, in order to reflect upon their relationship to the central core of his existence. In the
beginning Diederich's university days are described, and they afford the novelist a superb opportunity for merciless mockery of the aristocratic
clubs. In these circles Kaiser-worship is a
well-established cult, "Kaisertreue" has supplanted all other virtues, and incidentally, a war
with the debased nations, France and England, in
support of the Kaiser's principles, is looked upon
as definitely arranged. After the death of his
father, Diederich becomes the representative of
the family fortunes, the proprietor of a paper
factory, and, also by inheritance, takes a leading
position in the conservative circles of his native
town. A trial for *lèse-majesté* stands here in

the foreground, decked out with a mass of serio-comic details, and at preposterous length. Diederich's wedding journey, oddly enough, synchronizes with one of the Emperor's trips to Italy; this is a dainty morsel for the novelist, and he smacks his lips over its toothsomeness. The dedication of the Emperor William monument forms a telling end for the story; here the novelist gives free play to his satirical bent, and produces a little masterpiece of the mock-heroic. Naturally Mann vents his scorn not only on lick-spittle servility toward the very shadow of a monarch, but he jeers as well at every kind of toadyism; the life of a provincial community, organized and petrified in tradition, affords considerable scope for his merriment. The effect of the satire is not at all lessened by the fact that Diederich, with all his transparent idiocy, moves among his fellows with distinction, and is even a success in the manufacture of paper.

As a novel the book bristles with faults; only in the hands of a supreme genius can satire be thus sustained. But, as a contemporary document, perhaps comparable with the multitude of post-reformation screeds, it has real significance. That such a book could be written, and not by a professional socialist, before the fall of the Hohenzollerns, forms a curious item in the story of Germany's relation to Prussia's royal house. Mann had his companions in his liberalism, in his comprehension of the things that were.

Bernhard Kellermann's talents, though considerable, are still undisciplined. He resembles

a singer who is capable of reaching an extraordinarily high note, and is consumed with a
desire to prove this in season and out of season.
Yet his methods have produced in "Der 9te
November" one of the most memorable stories
of the decade. The situation demanded, it may
well be, an unrestrained, a sensational designer,
for a proper presentation of its qualities; a novelist, ordinarily regarded as over-fond of lurid
backgrounds and startling dissonances, could
hardly overdo the matter. The violence of con-
trasting colours was there waiting for the artist
capable of arranging them into an appropriate
pattern. Kellermann sets out to portray the life
of Berlin during the last year before the armistice.

At the centre of the story he places the family
of General von Hecht-Babenberg. The General
himself typifies all that was arrogant and narrow-minded in German militarism; "the General's
world was peopled by beings who wore uniforms
and whose burial was accompanied by a salvo,"
and "these beings moved in accordance with definite and immutable laws;" the rest of mankind
simply did not exist for him,—even in the last
years of the war when the privilege of his rank
and station still permits him to drive about in
his limousine, he does not see the starving women
or the crippled veterans who are spattered with
mud from his swiftly turning wheels. But the
General is by no means invulnerable. A mistaken
order which he issued early in the war had resulted in the needless and fruitless sacrifice of
many men; this circumstance has been used by

an old personal rival to banish him from the
western field of glory to a desk in the war office. Here he spends his days in faithful but irritated and dispirited service. And this is not
all; he is pursued relentlessly by a strange little
old man in a brown over-coat, the father of a
soldier whom his order has sent to death. This
personage dogs the general's footsteps, appears
with uncanny prescience at unexpected as well as
at wonted places of the General's daily or occasional visits. With pathetic insistence the old
man demands his son back again. The figure of
the old man represents perhaps a kind of per-
sonified conscience; it is improbable and theatrical, a transparent device of the sensationalist,
but the fact is that it is effective, and in a very
high degree. Through benevolent activities, such
as were increasingly expected of women of all
classes, the General's daughter Ruth is gradually
led from the sheltered confines of her traditions;
she falls eventually under socialistic influences,
loves a socialist agitator, and is lost to her father
and his class. In Otto, the General's son, Kellermann would apparently disclose the attitude of
many young officers toward the war in its last
stages; there is no longer any elation of spirit
in serving the cause of the fatherland, nor any
lingering impulse to high adventure; there is
nothing left on the western front but mud and
filth, and dead and living corpses. Into every
hour of one's furlough there intrudes the shattering consciousness that in so and so many hours
one will be in that earthly hell again. So Otto

in packing for his return, succeeds in arranging
a seemingly, accidental wound in his right hand,
and thus delays his departure.

Through the General's circle on the one hand,
and on the other, the world of the old man in
the brown over-coat, Kellermann contrives his
contrasts, though one might hesitate to decide
which is the more wretched. The most considerable female rôle is played by a certain Frau von
Dönhoff, a kind of Hetaira, whose festivals are
frequented by aristocratic and fastidious people.
The spirit of levity prevailing there, the sensuous
appeal of the arrangements and the general atmosphere of revelry, suggest that the novelist
intends to conjure up a scene of late Roman
voluptuousness. Other diversions in Berlin
lacked even the good taste with which Frau von
Dönhoff knew how to envelope her affairs. And
the lower classes can not even assume a covering
of gaiety; they are incapable of pretence; life is
to them soiled, vile, fetid, materially and spiritually. Only inertia or a traditional inhibition
prevents a universal suicide. A great capital,
once a city of dignity and beauty, though its
beauty was grandiose rather than winsome, a city
constantly scrubbed and combed into a pattern
of orderliness, an abode of joy and pleasure, however heavy-footed and graceless it often was, has
become a stagnant, slimy, ill-smelling pool. The
horses on the streets are skeletons; the dogs no
longer guard their masters' doors,—they have
served their masters in an unexpected way.
Children, hollow-eyed and narrow-chested, play

joyless games in ugly, unkempt alleys. Death has become so frequent that even to the children it has lost its holiness, its awe. On high and low the same intolerable weight presses down. The dust of far-away battle-fields stifles all. No one is capable of thinking any more; only animal characteristics remain, and those not even of the highest. All that was once held to be desirable and elevating, as worthy of one's devotion and self-sacrifice, has become a lie. The clouds sink down and usher in a "dusk of humanity" unparalleled in history.

Thus the German war novel represents the infinite variety of personal experience during the fatal years; every phase of personal opinion as to the conduct of the war, its origins, and its material and spiritual influence has found a voice in fiction. And the end is not yet. The type of novelist who uses fiction as a commentary on current events has not laid down his pen; he has only dipped it in another kind of ink. Thus one novelist paints a picture of merry Vienna in melancholy dilapidation and decay, another records fictitious happenings in the occupied zones —the question of the black troops in the Rhinelands has already its representative novel. As the definitive history of the war can not be written in our generation, so, it may be, the war will express itself conclusively in fiction only when one is farther removed from an insistent, benumbing personal relationship to it. There must be a process of emotional stabilizing before the great novel of the war can be written. Passion is not a function of intelligence; it may produce a perfect lyric, but great novels do not proceed from a section of the emotional organism which happens to be temporarily inflamed. Yet the ceaseless chatter about the war and the aftermath of war, is by no means contemptible or valueless. The war was one of the most momentous experiences through which the human race has passed, and sometime, a novelist learning to be faithful over a few things, may grasp the greater meaning of the experience in its entirety, and thus becoming master over many things, will write the great novel of the great war.

THE WAR UNHEEDED

A MAN whose house is burning would be
deemed erratic or demented if he displayed
indifference to the catastrophe. And yet, while
he devotes every energy to subduing the flames,
his inner spirit may be possessed by a calm satisfaction because he knows that his chief treasures
are not in the house at the time or are perhaps
preserved in fire-proof vaults. Or, to change
the figure, a man may whistle in passing through
a gloomy wood merely to embolden his own
spirit or to cheer his timid companions. These
two parables suggest the temper of many German novels of war times and after-war times,
which have nothing to do with the war or with
post-war adjustments. It is not easy in such
times to attain the "vantage ground of truth,—
a hill not to be commanded, and where the air
is always clear and serene,—and to see the errors, and wanderings, and mists, and tempests,
in the vale below," but some novelists have had
the courage to go on thinking about the timeless things, even when exultant crowds were
greeting a military victory, or rebellious mobs
were raiding butcher and baker.

Among war time novels which are not concerned with the war, Hauptmann's "Der Ketzer
von Soana" doubtless stands foremost. The
story is very brief, a hundred pages or thereabouts, and is told with that reserve, that de-
liberation, that effortlessness, which are the

marks of a great master. The scene is laid in
the part of Switzerland where rugged crags,—
one may perhaps say, the ascetic type of nature,
—slope toward the sun, and look on Italy. This
tilt of the physical world serves, it may be, as a
symbol for the content of the story. In this
region the narrator loves to wander. There he
hears the villagers tell of a strange hermit
dwelling up in the mountains, called "The Here-
tic of Soana," a man of exuberant vitality and
virility, filled with a contagious joy in living.
The story of this hermit is then fitted into the
framework which Hauptmann has prepared.

Francesco is a young priest in Soana. The
people learn to love him for his gentleness, his
kindliness, and his spiritual gifts, in time almost
to revere him as one close to sanctity. One day
a visitor bewilders him, a creature seemingly half
wild-man or mad-man, who stammeringly requests
that the children of his cottage be permitted to
attend the parish school. Francesco learns that
this family lives in a hut far up the mountain
slope, a brother and sister, with six children
whom popular rumour assigns to an incestuous
relation between them, though the woman herself maintains that the fathers in question were
so many wanderers in the mountains. The priest
goes to visit them in their outcast animalism.
Scarabota is himself really half-witted. He has
never heard of God, but he cherishes a little
image, a local fetish, the worship of which, apparently surviving from a forgotten tradition of
the mountains, recalls classic rites connected with

symbols of fertility and reproduction. The eldest
child is a maiden of rare beauty, a timid wild
thing, like a woodland faun or dryad. She does
not come to the service which Francesco holds
for these outlaws in a remote mountain chapel;
and in his search for her he finds shepherds and
goatherds who, temporarily at any rate, seem to
forget or ignore the dogmas of self-denial and
self-chastisement which are preached in the valley
below, and lead a joyful life of primitive simplicity, free as traditional satyrs or fauns. Sinful
thoughts fill the mind of the young priest; he can
not rid himself of them; confession and absolu-
tion bring no peace, no return to the old purity,
the old confidence. A mysterious new faith
seizes him, and gradually controls him entirely.
With this pariah, this leperous child of sin, he
forsakes his parish, goes forth to the heights,
and never returns.

Behind this brief story stand the antitheses
which Hauptmann chose nearly thirty years ago
as the theme for "Die versunkene Glocke" (The
Sunken Bell), the mountains with their freedom
and their joyfulness, and the valley with its restraints, its obligations, and its sour-faced inhibitions. Yet the book is not a propagandist
manifesto, urging a so-called rehabilitation of the
flesh, and perceiving in the doctrines of the
Church merely an undesirable and humanly impossible asceticism. The story is rooted in
Hauptmann's personality, the chief characteristic
of which is an all-embracing sympathy with human life in all its contradictions, an infinite pity

for human tears. Hauptmann began his literary
career in asking questions of our civilization, and
he has never wearied of the task. And all his
questions are variants of the single query, "Why
can not man be happy? Is it not possible to
reconcile a love of beauty, a joy in living, with
doctrines of self-discipline and moral responsibility?" But he does not imply a generalization
from the evidence which he presents; he simply
pleads with us to accompany him on his quest.

Hauptmann's latest story "Phantom" is a tale
of sin and subsequent regeneration of character.
The hero, who tells his own story, becomes
strangely infatuated with a young girl far above
his social and financial position. His passion
verges on madness, and the relation of his conduct becomes a powerful study in abnormal
psychology. He is led even to participation in
crime and suffers the penalty which is his due,
but the love of another woman, who becomes his
wife, and of her father, brings his soul to content and peace. The story can not deny a kinship
with Dostoievsky's "Crime and Punishment;" it
is, to be sure, a tiny canvas compared with the
Russian's great and sombre picture, yet within
its limits Hauptmann's book is not an unworthy
companion.

In perfection of workmanship, Arthur Schnitzler's "Casanovas Heimfahrt" (Casanova's Return Home) may perhaps take its place beside,
or at any rate, near to Hauptmann's little masterpiece, "Der Ketzer von Soana." From Casanova's memoirs Schnitzler takes the figure of the

famous adventurer, the hero of a thousand amorous affairs, the incomparable vagabond and swindler. In his own narrative, Casanova's exploits are like beads strung on a cord, one episode following another and forming, when taken together, a picaresque novel of prodigious size, but true to form in possessing no orderly development, no inevitable sequence. The modern novelist introduces a new element, the perceptible, but unacknowledged, or repudiated presence of mental and physical ageing. This lends an odd type of pathos to the story, an ennobling melancholy to an amorous quest. Sensuality is not thereby glorified or palliated, but the relation of it is refined.

Casanova was not accustomed to defeat in seeking a lady's favour, but he makes no progress with the fair Marcolina. He is driven to a subterfuge and impersonates the lady's lover in a nocturnal visit, a device common enough in the older comedy and novel. The culminating point in the narrative is reached in a duel with his rival, a conflict at early dawn between two naked men; this scene is an eighteenth century vignette of extraordinary beauty and delicacy. Though Casanova kills his antagonist, it is an idle and empty victory, closing the seemingly interminable line of his successes. The victor is really the vanquished, for he sees in the youthful form of his opponent the man he once was, is not now and never can be again; in the light of early morning he realizes the futility of his battle with the almighty years. Schnitzler's story is, to be

sure, only a single episode, but it reaches back
through the infinite vicissitudes of an extraordinary life for the sources of its peculiar power;
it concentrates the subtle forces of years in a
single day; it supplies a symbol of a universal,
poignant human experience. "Casanovas Heimfahrt" belongs perhaps among those novels whose
chief object was to entertain or divert in hours of
dejection or despair, but its merits as a narrative,
and, it may be, this little hint of that which sooner
or later, in one form or another, is man's inescap-
able destiny, lend it a far deeper significance.

Schnitzler's last story before the war was
"Frau Beate und ihr Sohn." A widowed mother
watches her son with anxious eyes; she is conscious of a particular peril which lies in wait for
him, the lure of an unscrupulous and erotic older
woman; but while seeking to guard him from
stain and disillusionment, she falls herself into
the deeps. "Doktor Gräsler," issued during the
war, is clever, but not important.

Sudermann's recent dramas have not been unmindful of the war, though one may question
whether these later plays add aught to his stature
as a dramatist. Indeed, there is some basis for
the opinion that Sudermann is really a novelist
who has been deflected from his natural course
by the glitter of a success in the theatre, a success which, it would seem, has been gained at
times by flimsy and meretricious devices. Thus
he has been hindered from a ripening of his
power and stopped in the search for deeper truth.
At all events, his recent volume of short stories

"Litauische Geschichten" (Lithuanian Stories) is the most important work which Sudermann has done in many years. As the title suggests, the novelist has returned to the scene of his early novels in his East Prussian homeland, though even there he has chosen a new and narrow field, the life of Lithuanian peasants who are living in Prussian territory. When one considers the tragic intensity, the grip on life, which mark "Frau Sorge," "Der Katzensteg," and "Es war," one may perhaps liken Sudermann to the hero of his play "Sodoms Ende;" he would seem to have fallen a victim to the sophistications of a modern metropolis; the failure of "Das hohe Lied" (The Song of Songs), his one novel after many years, provides a further bit of evidence to support this point. In his early novels, the East Prussian gentry or landed proprietors stand in the foreground. Despite their provincial remoteness, they are unmistakably a part of the great scheme of associated and organized interests which constitutes modern life, but in the recent stories he has intensified the aloofness from metropolitan conventionality; he has chosen to depict a peasant people in many ways more primitive than the country folk whom he had introduced as accessories in the earlier books.

There are four stories in the volume. Their substance is homely and everyday, save as tragic events, prompted by primitive passions, break in upon the seemingly commonplace. The relation is extraordinarily facile but simple, as befits the

subject, and without the subtlety, or perhaps
condescension which so often mars the chronicles
of the humble. By the simplicity and directness
of the narration, the restraint and severity in
telling even of violence and passion, one is reminded of the Icelandic sagas. The story of
"Miks Bumbullis" is perhaps the most notable
of the group. Miks is a light-hearted ne'er-do-
well, of great strength and physical attraction.
He kills an aged guard who stands in the way
of his poaching exploits, but a little girl, the
orphan granddaughter of the guard who by
chance was lying in the old man's lap, is un-
harmed. Suspicion falls on Miks, but he manufactures an alibi;—he had been spending the
night at the home of a certain widow, a brutal,
sensuous woman, known to be eyeing Miks with
favour. Miks gets a job, but he insists on caring
for the little girl. Later he marries the widow,
and still insists on taking the little girl with
him. Here the child is ill-treated, without
Miks's knowledge, and dies. Later, the wife,
grown jealous because of a niece who falls in
love with Miks, takes vengeance by denying
Miks's former alibi, charging him now with the
crime. He disappears; it is supposed that he
has vanished over the border into Russia, but
his vengeful wife feels sure that he will come
back to bring food to the child's grave; and he
does, thus falling again into the clutches of the
law. "Die Reise nach Tilsit" (The Trip to
Tilsit) is, as a story, hardly inferior. It is the
record of a fisherman and small land-owner on

the far Baltic coast. The wife of his youth grows old and pale beside him, and his physical self turns towards a vigorous, robust servant. On the protest of the wife's father, the offensive servant is dismissed, but that does not end the matter; the girl hangs about, and there are clandestine meetings. Finally the peasant and his wife start on a long projected trip to Tilsit, the great city where marvellous sights are to be enjoyed. It is the husband's purpose to arrange for an over-turn of the boat, save himself, and thus through a seeming accident, rid himself of the vexing problem. But in Tilsit, he begins to take pride in his wife's appearance, she seems a gentlewoman; the old love reawakens, and the passions of youth are renewed. On the trip back, the accident which had been planned as a part of the outward journey actually does take place, through the husband's negligence, not his intent, but the husband is drowned instead of the wife. Yet from this day, in due time, a child is born, to be the solace of coming years.

Jakob Wassermann is one of those who in the din of battle did not forget their dreams; one of his dreams, indeed, "Christian Wahnschaffe," has made him a literary figure of international renown. For twenty years and more, Wassermann has been seeking the foundations of happiness. Doubtless much of his quest seems purely negative; he puts up a sign-post to show that happiness is not to be found along a certain pathway; he strips from us coil after coil of the

complacent self-satisfaction which tradition has
wound about us.   Yet he does not indulge in
fiery polemics against those who point confidently
to false guide-posts; he is not one of the intolerant liberals.   Nor is he a sombre pessimist.
On the contrary he is convinced that the elements
which make up man, the bones and sinews, even
the flesh of his nature, may by some new arrangement of being, be transformed into a nobler
life.

Thus, naturally, Wassermann is fond of
characters who either out of a burning discontent,
or else obeying some unconscious impulse, re-
nounce their inheritance and grope toward a
realization of their higher selves.   In his first
novel "Die Juden von Zirndorf" (The Jews of
Zirndorf) he pictures a Jew who turns aside
from the crystallized nobilities and pettinesses of
his race, because he finds in them no principle of
life.   The heroine of "Die Geschichte der jungen
Renate Fuchs" (The Story of Young Renate
Fuchs), though quite unconscious of the nature
of her quest, is nevertheless impelled to go on
and on through a welter of experiences, even
through the deepest depths, because there is
within her that which refuses to be satisfied.   In
the colourful, brilliant "Alexander in Babylon,"
Wassermann tests the conventional standards of
success and finds them spurious measures of value.
Alexander conquers the world, but there is no
real substance in his achievement; his very accumulation of mighty victories is empty and

barren; and he dies unsatisfied, longing for something that is really worthy of his effort.

To Wassermann the acceptance of the things that are, simply because they are, is the beginning and end of error. The man who does not greet life with a persistent interrogation point forfeits his birthright, and the height of absurdity is to reverence the chains which tradition has forged upon us. Thus to him it was an interesting experiment to speculate upon the life of one who had no traditions, no prepossessions whatever. The story of Caspar Hauser is still after the lapse of a century a fascinating mystery. In 1828 a youth of eighteen or thereabouts wandered into Nuremberg; though, as it appeared later, he was possessed of a normal, even acute mind, it was at that time so undeveloped that he was hardly able to tell in broken vocables the few matters which made up the sum total of his past. Most of his life, so far as he remembered it, had been spent in a cell so tiny that he was unable to stretch out his limbs; and the one attendant, whom he called "He," was the only person whom he ever saw. The records of neighbouring princely houses were searched for material to account for Caspar through the creation of a toothsome scandal; he was even said to be the heir to the Bavarian throne. Once he was seriously wounded by a masked man, and after some years he was murdered. In many respects Caspar Hauser resembles Grimmelshausen's Simplicissimus, and Wassermann's interest in his hero depends on the

same essential material which, in the beginning
at any rate, led the older novelist, two centuries
and more ago, to create his fascinating fool.
His mind is a "tabula rasa" upon which impressions are to be made. The world of the Thirty
Years' War seems uglier than we are wont to
fancy it when tested by the gauge of Simplicissimus's innocence and faith, similarly Caspar
Hauser provides the balances by which the
modern world is weighed and found wanting.
Could not some better, nobler being be fashioned out of this receptive, untouched material?
But Caspar falls into the hands of those who
bungle the task, of those who are fanatics or
sceptics, who look on him as a specimen for ex-
hibition purposes, or as a deliberate impostor.
The unknown murderer simply takes this poor
human waif, this plaything of civilization, and
ends the footless struggle.

"Die Masken Erwin Reiners" (The Masks
of Erwin Reiner) presents an unlovely type, peculiarly characteristic of the sophisticated modern
world, and dissects it for our inspection and our
disapproval. Reiner is a cultivated egotist; he
sees in his fellowmen merely a variety of objects
which may be of passing value to him, providing
material for his interest or pleasure. The scene
is laid in Vienna, and the character of Erwin
Reiner has many points of contact with the Viennese Hofmannsthal's "Fool" in the little play
"The Fool and Death,"

"Der keinem etwas war, und keiner ihm."

Though begun several years before, "Das
Gänsemännchen" was not published till after the
outbreak of the war: this story shows a further
ripening of Wassermann's power both as a novelist and as a critic of contemporary society. He
presents here the devious ways by which a gifted
musician finds his real self, a harmony between
his inner life and his outward activity. There is
an English translation of "Das Gänsemännchen"
under the title, "The Goose Man."

Wassermann's earlier novels are in themselves
too important to be regarded as merely pre-
liminary studies for "Christian Wahnschaffe,"
but in a very real sense the great novel which
marks Wassermann's war-time activity, takes the
main threads of preceding works and weaves
them into a new and more splendid pattern.
They presented individually certain fragments of
life, essentially contemporaneous notwithstanding
the remoteness of "Alexander in Babylon" or of
"Caspar Hauser;" in the later novel Wassermann pieces the fragments together and forms
a picture of European society in pre-war days,
a picture of prodigious size and overwhelming in
its variety. The content of "Christian Wahnschaffe" is not easily reducible to a simple outline.
Christian belongs to a family of vast wealth;
every cultural advantage has been his from the
beginning; he moves freely and intimately in the
highest social circles of England and the conti-
nent. In addition, he is a youth of rare beauty
and charm; from his babyhood everyone has paid
homage to him; nothing has been able to harm

him or mar him.   Christian is a modern Balder,
a being of light.   The titles of the two volumes
of the novel, "Eva" and "Ruth," symbolize the
focus of Christian's interests in two periods.   Eva
is a celebrated dancer, an incomparable artist,
who holds the world in thrall.   In this atmosphere
of sensuous pleasure and sublimated æstheticism
Christian lingers for a time; but before other interests arise, he begins to perceive the limitations
of Eva herself and all that she represents.   In
Eva's beauty Christian can no more experience
enduring satisfaction than Faust could find the
moment of perfect bliss, even though Helen of
Troy was summoned from the realm of shades
to be his consort.   Later Eva becomes the mistress of a Russian Grand Duke and rolls in fab-
ulous magnificence; dabbling in international
intrigues, she is credited with influencing if not
controlling the destiny of nations.   Eventually
she is killed by an infuriated mob at her Kubla
Khan palace in the Crimea.   The final scenes of
Eva's career could safely be recommended to the
attention of cinema producers.   Ruth is a Jewish
girl in a Berlin tenement; in the midst of shadows
she walks in the light, giving light; in foulness
and meanness she remains without stain; her innocence can think no evil.   Notwithstanding her
Jewish blood and training, Ruth reads and re-
reads the New Testament; unconsciously she
fashions her very being after One who was all
unselfishness.   For a brief space she becomes the
lode-star of Christian's thinking.   The murder
of Ruth by a foul degenerate is one of the most

brutally awful passages in the whole range of modern fiction.

But long before meeting Ruth, Christian has renounced his family and turned his back on fashionable lotus-eating. In a house of ill repute at Hamburg, he encounters a wayward woman of the streets, already diseased in body, and treading the downward slope to death. He rescues her, takes her to Berlin, and supports her there till her death, as it were, seeking to atone to the individual for the wrongs done by his class to her class; for a little while he restores her to her lost humanity. And it is her brother who kills little Ruth. Even to this incredibly vile criminal, Christian's human interest and sympathy are not denied; he is not beyond the reach of the human heart. Gradually Christian is lost from sight; he requests that neither his family nor his proletarian friends in Berlin should seek him, but rumour reports his presence now and then here and there, where need and distress are tormenting the children of men. As has been repeatedly suggested, the figure of St. Francis of Assisi may have hovered before Wassermann's imagination when he created Christian Wahnschaffe.

A multitude of characters accompanies the protagonists. Chief among them perhaps is Bernhard Crammon, who guides Christian in his days of international pleasure-seeking. Crammon is the very archetype of aristocratic idler and parasite; he derives his income primarily from gambling, and spends his time as a decorative

guest at noblemen's houses from Scotland to
Russia. He cares not a whit for anything except
the satisfaction of his varied appetites. Crammon belongs to the same tribe as Erwin Reiner.
And then there is Amadeus Voss, the son of a
forester, with whom Christian used to play in
boyhood; when he appears later, he serves as a
kind of foil for Christian, developing into a selfish man of the world, as Christian has already
begun to leave the world behind him.

The defects of Wassermann's masterpiece are
in part inseparable from his plan; he has essayed
to paint an enormous panorama of contemporary
society. The immensity of the undertaking is
staggering, and only the firmest control of the
material can prevent such a work from falling
into confusion or even chaos; if no principles of
cohesion are supplied, the novel will fall into
separate units, merely tied together in a bundle.
Wassermann's success in his enterprise is astound-
ing, but it must be admitted that he has found
room for episodes which are very tenuously attached either to the story as such or to its
fundamental ideas; such, for example, are the
adventures of Crammon's natural daughter, Lä-
titia, particularly in her marriage to a South
American nabob. The book suffers also from an
exuberance of the imagination, which cloys at
times rather than impresses. Wassermann has
written a masterly book of self-analysis which he
calls "Mein Weg als Deutscher und Jude" (My
Way as German and Jew); in this he tries to
estimate the main elements of his being in the

directions indicated. His literary work betrays
at least one Jewish characteristic; the imagination of the Jew is grandiloquent, a survival doubtless of his Oriental origins; even though the
Jewish author grovels for a time in the back-yards
of realism, when his imagination takes wing, there
is something spectacular in its flight. Disraeli's
novels, "Coningsby" for example, have something
of this quality, which is obviously not always a
defect. Christian Wahnschaffe, the mortal upon
whom every conceivable gift has been bestowed,
is akin to the heroes of Oriental fable, and as
such, though he wins our interest and affection,
he is sometimes less real to us than the novelist
unquestionably wished him to appear. The
splendour which surrounds Eva Sorel seems to
belong also to Eastern legend; neither her beauty
nor the power which it secures for her seems altogether credible in our modern world.

Yet, in a day of satisfaction with small things,
a novelist has had the courage, the audacity, if
you will, to publish a novel of nine hundred
pages, simply because he needs that number to
carry out his purpose. There is real grandeur in
Wassermann's ambition, and it would be niggardly to deny a measure of grandeur to his accomplishment. The merit of a picture has, of
course, no essential relationship to its size;
Tintoretto's "Paradise" is less significant than the
three hand-breadths of Vermeer's "Woman at the
Casement." Though Wassermann's gigantic canvas be inadequate for a complete presentation of
contemporary civilization, it would be difficult to

name a single work of the creative imagination
which can compete with it. But the merit of the
novel does not lie in two dimensions alone. Wassermann penetrates into the complexities of a dis-
rupted, disheartened world, and he reduces it all
to a common denominator. And this common
principle which, as he sees it, lies at the very
root of all our illnesses, had already been indicated by the sub-title of "Caspar Hauser,"—
"Die Trägheit des Herzens," sloth of the heart.
Ruth, the little Jewish girl, living the teachings
of the New Testament, has found the solution of
life's riddle. An English translation of "Christian Wahnschaffe" bears the title "The World's
Illusion."

Gabriele Reuter participated in the production
of war fiction with a rather indifferent story
called "Die Herrin" (The Lady of the Manor).
The heroine is an aged aristocrat, the owner of
a vast, half feudal domain in the region of the
Harz Mountains. She is a personage of incredible unloveliness and brutality; she fascinates
through the limitless ugliness of her character.
The main conflict of the story is between this incomparable old vixen and the second wife of her
grandson, whose first wife, by the way, she has
worried to death. This second granddaughter-
in-law is a modern woman, not by any means to
be intimidated, and jealous of the last word.
The elements of this picturesque contest are in
part supplied through the events of the great
war.

Far more significant is another novel by Gabriele Reuter, "Die Jugend eines Idealisten"
(The Youth of an Idealist), published during
the war years, but in no way connected with its
specific problems. It shows certain points of interesting resemblance to Wassermann's great
novel. In several previous stories the novelist
had discussed some concrete theme of family relationship,—the woman married to a man outside
of her world, "Ellen von der Weiden," which
seemed somewhat like a modernized version of
Auerbach's once well-thumbed story "Die Frau
Professorin," the unmarried mother, in a very
venturesome book, "Das Tränenhaus" (The
House of Tears), the widow's relationship to
her sons as they grow beyond her feminine
guidance in "Frau Bürgelin und ihre Söhne." In
the new novel Gabriele Reuter investigates two
themes, skilfully allowing the earlier problem to
prepare the way for the second. The first of
these is an interesting variation of the problem
presented in the story of Frau Bürgelin and her
sons; here the mother becomes acquainted with
a grown son whom she has not seen since his
babyhood. She had left her husband, a country
gentleman, because of his unfaithfulness; this step
involved her abandoning her baby boy, and she
has later become an actress of great distinction.
Now on entering the university and incidentally
asserting his independence, the youth comes to
live with his mother and to participate for a
time in the affairs of her world. One is reminded of Anselma Heine's poignant story "Eine

Peri," in which a great singer takes her grown
children to herself and fancies that she is at last
to have a "home." With rare delicacy Gabriele
Reuter presents the situation,—the belated, un-
fed mother-love after all these years, the ardour,
the curiosity, and at times the disillusionment of
the son. With fine insight she contrasts the relationship of this mother and son to one another,
an acquaintance gained through conscious effort
and mature observation, with the unconscious
growth of normal family life. There is a
curiously fascinating detachment, abnormal but
in the circumstances inevitable, in the attitude of
mother and son to each other. But the hero is
satisfied neither in the brilliant social life of
Berlin to which his own aristocratic connections
or his mother's fame assure him access, nor in the
university companionships of an exclusive club,—
its obligations are irksome and its merriment re-
pulsive or empty. He learns to know a totally
different world of work and woe, and turning
his back on social position and inherited privilege,
he goes to live among the poor and wretched.
A great idea takes possession of him, and he
devotes his life to gaining acceptance for it
among the younger generation; he seeks to stim-
ulate wholesome relationships between young
men and young women, to teach young men to
look upon womankind in a different way, no
longer as mere objects of evil lust, but as comrades and sisters; the book becomes a plea for
pre-marriage purity among young men. To this
cause the hero dedicates his life after the tragic

disclosure that a girl whom he has loved with boyish devotion and manhood's ardour is really the daughter of his own father.

Whatever may or may not have been Germany's ambitions for world dominion, the war gradually erected barriers of brass about the fatherland. Beyond these barriers indeed the imagination at times took flight to scenes remote in time and place from the war-tortured lands of western Europe. Eduard Stucken's massive and impressive novel "Die weissen Götter" (The White Gods), for example, found new romance in the old story of the Spanish conquerors in Mexico. But in general, perhaps, the disappointment in the great experiment of outward activity led to introspection, or to a solemn scrutiny of the spiritual possessions which could never be made part of a material indemnity. Thus many novelists sought relief, perhaps a finer thing, a solace, in a return to the soil; though, it may be remarked, some had never left it. The novel of country or provincial life to which the Germans have applied the term "Heimatkunst" has shown a renewed vitality. In their very essence, stories of this type differ from the novel of "local colour." The latter is often simply the novelist's exploitation of matters which by chance or conscious enterprise have become familiar to him and may possess a factitious interest largely because they are unfamiliar to others. Often the use of "local colour" is a clever covering for paucity of the inventive imagination or an inability to grasp anything

deeper than picturesque superficialities. No
novel can depend on "local colour" for its higher
values. Novels of "Heimatkunst" seek a deepening of human life in the present by calling attention to the heritage of uninterrupted tradition.
In a very real sense they insist and try to de-
monstrate that the people of a certain community
have grown from the soil; the land which bears
them has become bone of their bone, flesh of
their flesh. "We were about to sell our inheritance for a mess of pottage," these novelists now
seem to be saying, "the finger of fate has in-
terposed; let us go back and inspect the old home
which we were exchanging for a bogus palace."
And so they focus our attention on the homely
virtues, the sturdy manliness, the healthy solidity
of peasant and yeoman; they lead us to the abiding simplicities of country vicarage and school-
room, and tell us of the riches which the war has
left untouched. The novels of Hermann Löns
are good examples of this return to nature; Löns
himself was killed early in the war, and the later
recognition of his merits is witness to the increasing appreciation for this type of story. Even
when the work is strongly touched with sentiment,
as in the "Heide" novels of Felicitas Rose, it still
rings true.

It may, at first thought, seem a far cry from
such novels to the stories of Count Eduard
Keyserling; but the latter are born of the same
impulse, simply translated into another sphere.
The life that he knows and loves, equally rooted
in an ancestral soil, Count Keyserling portrays

with mellow art and great charm; he is the novelist of the East Prussian nobility. And with quiet dignity he continued on his pathway; the war did not turn him aside, though one may imagine the ageing nobleman watching its progress with aching heart, for it was pulling the house of his forefathers down over his very head. Yet in the midst of the war, in the story "Fürstinnen" (Princesses) he produced his ripest, his most artistic work. It was doubtless a mere corner of life which he made his own; it was a system of living, long outworn, which perhaps merited our disapproval and deserved its fate, but Keyserling invests it with a wistful beauty, the after-glow when the sun has set.

The same return to a traditional idealism is attested by the increased popularity of Waldemar Bonsels's stories; it is merely a different aspect of the same impulse. The best of Bonsels's work is a kind of modern counterpart of the old folk-tales, the possession of which has already given the German people a joyous reassurance in a time of national depression. Bonsels is a lover of nature, and seeks an interpretation of human life through reference to the natural world. There is of course nothing essentially new in Bonsels's approach. Maeterlinck, Fabre and many others, have endowed the animal world, or the insect world, with sentient, purposeful, moral living. Bonsels is a man of delicate sensibilities; he unites rare poetic fancy with moral earnestness, and creates for spider, bee, and house-fly a life of conscious will-power, tastes, ambitions,

and ethical standards. This is the way in which
the immortal fairy-tales once came into being.
Bonsels's little story "Die Biene Maja" (Maja
the Bee) was, to be sure, published before the
outbreak of the war, but only gradually has it
attained the dignity of a contemporary classic.
It is a modern fairy-tale for children of all ages.
If one really insists on seeing social or political
satire in the adventures of the baby bee, one may
test the tale from that point of view and is, incidentally, quite welcome to the results of the
investigation.

This search for ideal bases of living, this re-
inspection of abandoned standards, has in recent
years made the religious novel a more common
phenomenon in the book market than it was ten
years ago. Of this tendency Rudolf Hans
Bartsch's reverent little book "Er; Ein Buch der
Andacht" (He: a Book of Worship) is an
example. Bartsch assumes that Christ did not
die upon the cross, and invents a series of later
experiences, mainly in Rome. But the martyr's
death is not lacking; Christ protests against in-
human treatment of a poor beast, and is Himself
in derision harnessed to a cart to help the animal
in drawing it, dying under the blows which are
now transferred to Him. One may mention also
Ouckama Knoop's religious novel "Das A und
das O" (The Alpha and the Omega), written
before the war but not published till later, un-
orthodox perhaps but essentially devout, and
even Max Brod's thoughtful nonconformity in

"Tycho Brahes Weg zu Gott" (Tycho Brahe's Road to God).

In emphasizing an idealistic trend in contemporary fiction, it may seem like stretching a point to include reference to a number of novels which portray certain abnormal or diseased human relationships. One may contend that such matters belong in the psychopathic ward, and that the discussion of them should be confined to medical treatises. This may well be. Yet the authors of these books are not necessarily pandering to a depraved taste and a morbid curiosity; it would seem that in some cases they are genuinely prompted by an honest desire to study the nature of man, what sort of being is he? are there not hidden recesses of his character which must be understood, before he can attain to that more perfect adjustment of his being which is possible here and now?

In spite of considerable capable, honest work, and two or three novels of distinguished merit, the harvest of the last years has been meagre. Patriotism, so it seems, is in literature one of the most sterile of emotional stimuli; this may be said of nationalism in the narrower sense without danger of contradiction. And much of German emotional life has been absorbed, directly or indirectly, in the exercise of these faculties. Some of the most notable practitioners in fiction have passed these years in silence, virtual or complete. Ricarda Huch, for example, with all her superb talents, has for a decade and more written only one novel, and that merely an account of a trial

for murder, "Der Fall Deruga" (The Deruga
Case). The story is, to be sure, highly entertaining, is skilfully conceived, humorous, facile in
execution, and in the character of Dr. Deruga
the novelist has created an original personality
of commanding fascination and interest. In dis-
heartening times the novelist sought, it may be,
a pastime for herself and a diversion for others.
Possibly she had not the heart to take up some
deeper problem of our humanity, or to dream
one of her iridescent dreams. She has indeed in
the meantime written a volume on the religious
beliefs of Luther and a book of reverent and
penetrating meditations on the Bible;—these are
not to be despised, but one longs for another
"Ludolf Ursleu" or "Michael Unger." One
may say much the same of Thomas Mann. His
"Buddenbrooks," published in 1901, remains one
of the outstanding achievements of the new
century; it is a novel built four-square, one may
say, with a breadth and solidity which remind
one of the great Russians. A little later, in "Der
Tod in Venedig" (A Death in Venice) he treated
an unusual and unattractive theme with great discretion and with finished art. In recent years, to
be sure, he has not been a negligible figure in
German thought; his essays on political and social topics must be reckoned with, and his little
study "Herr und Hund" (Master and Dog)
is also worth a passing mention. In times of
turmoil and disillusionment, Mann finds his dog
a more reliable, a more interesting companion
than his fellowmen. A dog, racially a very ordi-

nary mongrel beast, is here the subject of pains-
taking and loving observation; in him the author
has created a character, and the literature of the
dog has been materially enriched. Yet with the
years, one desires another novel to place on the
shelf beside "Buddenbrooks."

The silence of those whom we have liked to
hear is a disappointment, but far more depress-
ing is work which betrays a loosening of the artistic conscience. Fifteen years ago Georg Hirschfeld published a novel which was not merely a
promise but was a decidedly distinguished per-
formance, "Der Wirt von Veladuz." Similarly
Georg Hermann's "Jettchen Gebert" was both
conceived and executed on a very high level of
excellence; not only did it afford an unequalled
picture of Berlin in the thirties, the "Bieder-
meier" period, but it unfolded a touching and
powerful story of inter-racial relationship, Jew
and Gentile, the equal of which it would not be
easy to name. But for a decade neither Hirschfeld nor Hermann has approached the standard
which they set for themselves, and, it must be
confessed, they have in various instances seemed
quite ignobly content with inferior wares. In
the first decade of the new century Rudolf Herzog gave evidence of genuine abilities. "Die
Wiskottens" and "Die Hanseaten," for example,
betokened power in the one case to grasp a modern industrial situation and involve it memorably
in a story, in the other to present with sincerity
and completeness the portrait of a place, the
outer life and the inner soul of Hamburg. Yet

recent products have shown little sustained power
and have been corroded with sentimentalism.

It would seem also that the reputation of
Rudolf Hans Bartsch was founded on the
sands; one may doubt that he ever merited the
welcome which he once received. To-day we may
surmise that a part of his renown was due to his
uncompromisingly German attitude in a district
where the German language and German things
in general were waging a ceaseless war with another tongue and another culture; his position as
a borderland propagandist was confirmed by the
novel "Das deutsche Leid" (The German Sorrow). His little war story "Der Flieger" (The
Aviator) begins admirably; an aviator in the
Austrian service is driven to earth in the midst
of a sparsely populated woodland district in
Serbia; here Bartsch works for a time very effectively with a situation of the Crusoe type, but luck
and sentiment soon take possession of the story
and run away with it. Notwithstanding his genuine narrative talent and a certain grace of manner, Bartsch's novels are at bottom thin and theatrical. The position of the Swiss novelist J. C.
Heer seems in part built on similar foundations;
in it the influence of patriotic prepossessions is
manifest: Heer is a German Swiss, ardently anti-
Italian in a region where the two cultures meet.

It may, of course, be readily admitted that the
literary life of Germany is at present peculiarly
active. Newer talents have come to the fore in
considerable numbers and have insisted that they
have something to say and that there are even

interesting new ways of saying the age-old things. Among the newer story-tellers, Rudolf Binding and Wilhelm von Speyer may be mentioned, real masters of the craft, to whose later development one can look with confidence. The work of the innovators also commands the attention of all who are not repelled by youthful audacity or who acknowledge the possibility of new forms. Experimentation and eccentricity, or what to-day seems like eccentricity, mark much of the new work, and the terms which have now become familiar when applied to painting are equally applicable to literature. Yet the literature of new adventure in theory or form has chosen the drama and the lyric as its chief methods of expression rather than the novel or the short story.

In the last years Carl Sternheim has gained a considerable notoriety by his cynical, supercilious thrusts at bourgeois society and through the innovations of his artificially laboured and crabbed style. The latter is not an entirely uninteresting experiment; Sternheim seeks to express himself concretely without rhetorical figures, and to reduce his sentences to the essential elements, even in defiance of traditional syntax. His stories, such as "Fairfax," a biting post-war satire with an American multi-millionaire as protagonist, or the dozen or more sketches which make up his "Chronik von des zwanzigsten Jahrhunderts Beginn," possess undeniable merit as transcripts of reality minutely observed, but they are for the most part nervous, brutal, and trivial, with a slant in the direction of the abnormal and perverse.

Franz Werfel is doubtless one of the outstanding figures of the generation; the new cult of "expressionism," with its interesting theories and its by no means negligible experiments, sees in him a most gifted representative. Though his work lies mainly in other fields, Werfel has written one memorable novel, "Nicht der Mörder sondern der Ermordete ist schuld" (Not the Murderer but the Murdered Man is Guilty). There is, however, nothing radical or novel in the story, though its psychological bases, its fine discriminations of inner motives, perhaps even its sense of awe-filled mystery in the connection between thought and deed, between one man's thought and another man's deed, are to be associated both with recent speculations as to the working of men's minds and with an honest though intensely modern recognition of the inadequacy of all our philosophies.

Kasimir Edschmid, also a high priest of "expressionism," has essayed the novel, but in his chief effort "Die achatenen Kugeln" (The Agate Beads) he has hardly progressed beyond the stage of conscious rebellion and protest, and has achieved merely a stylistic oddity. The style is abrupt, staccato, incredibly condensed, a single paragraph often containing material for many chapters. The book seems at times like the rough notes for a story or rather a score of stories, jotted down incoherently, an unbelievable accumulation of detail. The novelist without doubt had no intention of presenting coherence and harmony, since he sees neither the one nor the other in life, and it is his purpose to give life in its entirety. One suspects, however, that the un-blushing details of hospital routine, for example, or the minutiæ of erotic rendezvous are not in-serted honestly to complete the picture of life, but as examples of the novelist's virtuosity, if in-deed a less worthy motive is not also lurking in the background. Otto Flake may be classed as an "expressionist," though to the theories of his fellows he adds some peculiar corollaries of his own. Flake holds that the new novel must aban-don the concrete for the abstract, and he likens his canvases to the work of the Cubists; he is of the opinion also that the new type of novel must avoid the consecutive principle of narration, characteristic of older fiction, and must relate the "simultaneous," a theory, incidentally, which Karl Gutzkow advanced now nearly a century ago. The chief examples of his art, "Die Stadt des Hirns" (The City of the Brain) and "Nein und Ja" (No and Yes) are, through the identity of the leading characters, practically one novel. Effort is made to reduce character and conduct to abstract terms; as specimens of this endeavour one may note the eight detailed character analyses supplied for cer-tain acquaintances of the hero, who are desig-nated by the first eight letters of the alphabet; conduct for the most part refuses to become ab-stract and must be accounted for through narra-tive elements of the traditional type. The novel-ist apparently seeks to attain simultaneity by the odd device of intercalated narratives, which in part are told within one another, like a Chinese nest of boxes. The story which these novels relate, with its war time backgrounds, is by no means uninteresting or insignificant, but it is buried under an incredible mass of pretentious philosophical and metaphysical discussion, and Flake's fundamental principles will seem to most readers merely a foolish handicap upon his real talent as a narrator. Edschmid and Flake have certainly not as yet developed the expressionistic novel into a recognizable genre. Naturally the expressionists and the post-expressionists of the next few years may mould the novel into an instrument of their purposes, and a new type of novel may be born. One can only wait and see.

INDEX

INDEX OF AUTHORS AND TITLES

Index 291